Matthew M. Vriends, PhD

Gouldian Finches

Everything about Purchase, Housing, Care,
Nutrition, Breeding, and Diseases

With a Special Chapter on Understanding
Gouldian Finches

With 22 Color Photographs

Drawings by Michele Earle-Bridges

BARRON'S

Photos on Covers:
Front cover: Left, a white-breasted mutation; center, a yellow Gouldian; right, a yellow- or orange-headed Gouldian.
Inside front cover: normal black-headed Gouldian.
Inside back cover: yellow-headed white-breasted yellow Gouldian finches.
Back cover: Above left: black-headed Gouldian. Above right: white-breasted red-headed male. Below: left, orange-headed Gouldian, right, white-breasted red-headed male.

All inquiries should be addressed to:
Barron's Educational Series, Inc.
250 Wireless Boulevard
Hauppauge, NY 11788

International Standard Book No. 0-8120-4523-8

Library of Congress Catalog Card No. 90-19771

Library of Congress Cataloging-in-Publication Data

Vriends, Matthew M., 1937–
    Gouldian finches : everything about purchase, housing, care, nutrition, breeding, and diseases : with a special chapter on understanding Gouldian finches / Matthew M. Vriends : drawings by Michele Earle-Bridges.
        p.   cm.
    Includes bibliographical references (p.   ) and index.
    ISBN 0-8120-4523-8
    1. Gouldian finch.   I. Title.
    SF473.G68V75   1990   90-19771
    636.6'862 — dc20   CIP

Printed in Hong Kong

5 6 7 8   4900   9 8 7 6

About the author:
Matthew M. Vriends is a Dutch-born biologist/ornithologist who holds a collection of advanced degrees, including a PhD in zoology. Dr. Vriends has written more than 80 books in three languages on birds and other animals; his detailed works on parrotlike birds and finches are well known. Dr. Vriends has traveled extensively in South America, the United States, Africa, Australia, and Europe to observe and study birds in their natural environment and is widely regarded as an expert in tropical ornithology and aviculture. A source of particular pride are the many first-breeding results he has achieved in his large aviaries, which house more than 50 tropical bird species. Dr. Vriends and his family live near Cincinnati, Ohio. He is the author of two of Barron's Pet Owner's Manuals, *Lovebirds* and *Pigeons*, of Barron's Complete Nature Lover's Manual, *Feeding and Sheltering Backyard Birds,* and of two of Barron's Pet Owners Handbooks, *The New Bird Handbook* and *The New Cockatiel Handbook.*

Photo credits: Andy Cohen (Cohen Associates)/birds courtesy of Valerie Fellerman: page 28 above left, below left; page 64 below; inside back cover; back cover above left.
Edward M. Czarnetzky: page 10 above; page 28 above right, below right.
Terry Dunham (Avian Genetics Company): page 10 bottom right; page 46; page 63; page 64 above.
Paul Kwast: inside front cover; page 10 below left.
B. Everett Webb (Nature's Moments Photography): front cover; page 9; page 27; page 45; back cover above right, below.

Important note:
    The subject of this book is how to take care of Gouldian Finches in captivity. In dealing with these birds, always remember that newly purchased birds — even when they appear perfectly healthy — may well be carriers of salmonellae. This is why it is highly advisable to have sample droppings analyzed and to observe strict hygienic rules. Other infectious diseases that can endanger humans, such as ornithosis and tuberculosis, are rare in many pet birds. Still, if you see a doctor because you or a member of your household has symptoms of a cold or of the flu, mention that you keep birds. No one who is allergic to feathers or feather dust should keep birds.
    Most food insects are pests that can infest stored food and create a serious nuisance in our households. If you decide to grow any of these insects, be extremely careful to prevent them from escaping from their containers.

Contents

Contents

Preface

The first living Gouldian finches to arrive in England in 1887 created a sensation; a similar reaction to these colorful birds occurred in Berlin in 1896–1897, when they were introduced to the public at a large bird exhibition.

There is no doubt that these birds, with their remarkably colored plumage, can be accepted as the most beautiful of the finches and have always created an interest to the bird loving public. The colors that these birds exhibit almost border on the unnatural. It is no wonder that, as I discovered and frequently heard during my study trips, Australian aviculturists refer to them as "the king of all finches." Unfortunately, aviculturists "down under" as well as their colleagues in other parts of the globe, often refer to them as a "problem bird" — a name that holds a certain degree of authenticity for, over the years, these birds have indeed posed various husbandry and breeding problems. Happily, generations of dedicated bird keepers have experimented by trial and error to reduce these problems that are now not nearly so serious. However, the Gouldian Finch still is not recommended for the beginners and should only be acquired by people with previous avicultural experience. Beginners should first gain experience with hardier birds such as zebra finches or Bengalese (also known as society finches) before venturing onto more ambitious projects where the possibilities of failure and disappointment cannot be discounted. The fancier who has a desire for Gouldians should first thoroughly acquaint himself with them through avicultural societies, literature, and so on.

Nevertheless, the Gouldian finch is one of the most satisfying cage or aviary birds, providing of course, that one ensures the bird gets all it requires to keep it in top condition.

The owner of a pair of acclimatized Gouldian finches that are in top condition will soon discover how trusting they are. After a few weeks in a roomy cage or an indoor or garden aviary, and when they are accustomed to their new surroundings, the birds will remain "unflappable," even when you provide them with fresh food and water, providing you treat them with the respect they deserve. If you approach your birds with calmness and kindness, they will respond in a similar manner.

Gouldian finches then, are in every respect excellent birds to keep in cage or aviary. At the present time they are extremely popular, due in part to the many fascinating color mutations that have been developed in various parts of the world over the last 35 years, although it is not always possible to assess which rules of heredity apply to some varieties. Luckily however, the most important mutations are well documented and these are discussed fully in this book. In addition, there is comprehensive information on the particular diseases contracted by Gouldians as well as full coverage of housing, care, management, and breeding.

This book, therefore, will be an indispensable guide to all beginning aviculturists with an interest in Gouldian finches. It also will be of interest to those already experienced with these colorful birds, although some readers may not necessarily agree (and that is not a bad thing!) with all of my ideas. If there is a dynamic hobby — it is definitely aviculture!

I would like to thank my friend and colleague John Coborn for taking so much work off my hands, my wife Lucia Vriends-Parent for her ongoing assistance in the compilation of this book, J. Peter Hill, DVM for reviewing the manuscript and making valuable contributions to the text, and the many bird lovers at home and abroad who, over the years, have provided me with the results of their experiences. However, any shortcomings in the text can only be my own responsibility.

As always, I will be grateful for any comments or constructive criticism on the contents of this book.

Loveland, Ohio   Matthew M. Vriends
Summer 1990

Soyons fidèles à nos faiblesse.
For Kimberly, my first grandchild.

Buying Gouldian Finches

Gouldian finches should never be acquired until the accommodations for them are fully sited, prepared, and furnished (see pages 14 and 15). It also is important that you are thoroughly prepared to offer the best care and management, especially with regard to temperature and humidity (page 14). Only after all this has been done and you know precisely what you are doing should you go to purchase the birds.

Obtaining Quality Gouldian Finches

How do I ensure I get only the best birds? This must be considered carefully; we are talking about relatively expensive birds and want to minimize all risks.

Other Gouldian Breeders

If you are a member of a bird society (which is very desirable), then you will have the advantage of being able to see your colleagues' finches. Experienced Gouldian owning members especially, will be able to put you on the right track. In any case it is a good idea to visit a few Gouldian breeders and see how they operate. Look at the cages and aviaries; see what kind of food is being given; check the breeding records if you can — all good Gouldian breeders keep detailed records of their work. Anyone who tries to breed the birds randomly without proper care will not be very successful. He also will not be able to answer certain questions such as: Are the parents good brooders? Do they feed their young regularly and adequately? Did the young develop normally? A breeder who gives negative answers to these questions may be a ''fancier'' only in the fact that he thinks he is going to make a lot of money. I think it is not necessary to advise you to go elsewhere.

The best breeders are thus those who not only have a good collection of healthy, tightly plumaged birds, but also can show you breeding records of all their breeding pairs (and their offspring). Should you wish to breed particular mutations at a later date, it is essential that you are aware of the genetic makeup of the adults and their offspring and that you know as much as possible about ancestors.

Serious breeders also should ring their birds with the so called closed-bands available from a society. All concerned will then know the age of the bird and whether it is suitable for breeding. When purchasing birds, examine the leg band, which will show the breeding number of the breeder and the year of the breeding. *Never buy birds that are not close banded.* Also it is not advisable to buy birds more than three years of age as they are unlikely to be good breeders.

It is also advisable to buy young birds that have

Knowing the different parts of a bird's body is especially useful when talking with breeders, judges, and avian veterinarians.
1. crown 2. forehead 3. upper mandible 4. lower mandible 5. chin, malar region, and throat 6. jugulum and breast 7. front toes 8. hind toe 9. tibia 10. undertail-coverts and cloaca 11. outertail feathers 12. upper-tail coverts 13. rump 14. bend of wing and shoulder 15. back 16. nape

fully completed the first molt and are in their first adult plumage. Experience has shown that birds moved to a new environment before the first molt are more susceptible to stress and its possible attendant diseases. In such cases do not take any risks! Some birds may still carry a few signs of juvenile plumage even after the first molt, especially on the head and neck; however this will disappear fully after the second molt so we will not need to worry unduly about it.

I would like to discuss two more possibilities appertaining to the acquisition of Gouldian finches:

Pet Stores

Today many pet stores are able to supply some excellent bird material. The pet shop staff usually is well informed (they really *must* be, although this unfortunately is not always the case) or may be enthusiastic bird breeders in their own right. Pet stores also receive many birds from breeders in their own areas and, if conscientious enough, the proprietors only will obtain stock from breeders with a good name, a name that they should not try to keep from a prospective client. Indeed, a client should be encouraged to visit the breeder to see how his livestock is cared for and accommodated.

If purchasing birds from a pet shop, the rules still apply: only accept birds with closed leg-bands and that are at least through the first molt. If you seriously require genetical information about the birds, then the pet shop should have access to breeding records. Examine the birds in which you are interested; first from a distance, and see if they are sufficiently active. A bird that sits moping in a corner with its feathers puffed out should not be purchased. Take a prospective purchase in the hand and gently blow its breast feathers to one side; its breastbone should not stick out like the blade of a knife (see How to Tell Sick Gouldian Finches from Healthy Ones, pages 7–8).

If you buy birds from a pet shop, only buy young birds that have completed the first molt and are now good in adult plumage without bare patches, especially on the neck or breast. They should, naturally, have not yet bred.

If you buy older birds, you will no doubt inherit the headaches of their breeder.

Friends

If you buy Gouldians from a friend who has successfully bred them, ask to see the parent birds. If these are fit and healthy and the youngsters strong and nimble; then you can buy without any qualms.

How to Tell Sick Gouldian Finches from Healthy Ones

The birds that we buy must be as fit as a fiddle. In the chapter on diseases (page 47) we discuss in detail the diseases that Gouldians are likely to suffer from. But, in order to avoid many problems later we must first buy healthy birds. The following is a list of important points to be considered when purchasing birds:
• There should be no discharge from the eyes.
• The eyes should be clear and bright (normal Gouldian eyes are dark brown, somewhat lighter in juveniles).
• During the day, birds should not sit sleeping with closed eyes on a perch — later they may tuck the head under the wing and gasp for breath.
• There should be no swellings around the eyes.
• There should be no nasal discharge; the nostrils should be free and clear.
• The head feathers, especially those around the beak, should not be soiled (which can happen if a bird with nasal discharge continuously wipes its beak on a perch).
• The bird should not palpitate, pant, or sneeze.
• The bird should not sit continuously by the seed hopper and make more mess than eat. A bird that picks up a seed without dehusking it and eating it, then letting it drop, has no appetite.

Buying Gouldian Finches

As soon as a bird falls sick, it loses its bloom, its song, its activity, and its keen look. Its feathers will fluff out, it will sleep or sit hunched up in some corner, and may spend more time than usual at the feed dish.

• The bird should be tightly feathered and not fluffed-up with drooping wings; in such circumstances the bird will neglect preening and feather maintenance.
• A bird should continually use its voice; a silent bird often is failing in something or other.
• A bird must not be so thin that its breastbone sticks out like the blade of a knife—there is a danger that such a bird will waste virtually away to nothing. There must also be no lumps or masses on the body; such cases will require immediate veterinary treatment.
• A bird should have no balance problem; this often will indicate a serious condition that urgently requires veterinary treatment.
• A bird should not sit continually in some corner of a cage or aviary. Healthy birds will use a perch.
• A bird must not have thin and copious droppings (in this case, a vet must also be consulted).
• A resting bird should not sit on its perch with its beak open; such a bird should be referred to a vet.

• A bird should not have an overgrown or crossed beak as this will cause difficulty later when it comes to feed its young—such birds are seldom able to rear young satisfactorily.
• A bird must have good feet with no toes missing; incomplete feet pose difficulties during pairing.
• A bird should not limp or show unwillingness to use a foot (remember that roosting birds often sit on one foot only; a bird that is not quite in order may rest continually on both feet and this is often one of the first signs that all is not in order).
• A bird must not "pump its tail," that is to say the tail moves rhythmically back and forth, while the bird is otherwise "resting" on a perch or in a corner of cage or aviary.
• A bird must not show any bleeding—for whatever reason. A bleeding bird requires urgent veterinary attention.
• A bird that is older than three years is good for perhaps one more breeding season and really is better not purchased unless you urgently require it for particular genetical reasons. Birds in juvenile plumage also should be refused until after the first molt; disappointments and losses sometimes occur in the period when the young get their first adult plumage.

Transporting Gouldian Finches

We have just discussed the importance of selecting only the fittest and healthiest birds for our own collections. One of the most important conditions that must be kept to an absolute minimum is *stress* (see page 12).

All birds experience stress during capture and transport. Birds must be caught up with the greatest possible care, whether in the hand (as in a cage) or in a short-handled, fine-meshed net (for

The white-breasted mutation, which is recessive to the ▶ wild or normal forms, first appeared in Australia in 1954, and in South Africa and England in the late 1950s. The first specimens were imported into the United States shortly thereafter.

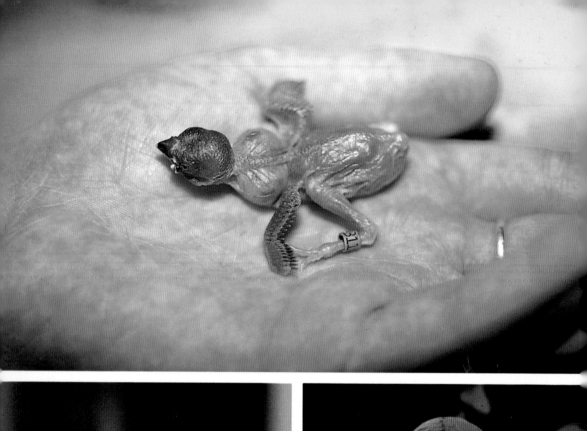

Buying Gouldian Finches

If a bird interests you, take it in your hand. Blow aside some breast feathers and check that the breast is "meaty" and full. Look at the legs, which should be smooth, not scaly. The beak should look normal and the eyes should be clear and bright.

aviary birds); in the latter case a single bird (never two or more at once) is "scooped" out of the air. First, remove all obstacles that can get in the way during catching. Never catch birds for longer than five minutes otherwise they will become too exhausted. Also, try and catch up in the smallest area, for example, in the night shelter of the aviary. Moreover, if catching up a number of birds to bring inside for the winter, for example, do it in several attempts, with "rest periods" in between. In general, the morning hours are the best time for catching up birds, so that they have the rest of the day to "recover"; for, believe me, they hate it!

The next step is the transport of the birds. If we are referring to a short, half-hour journey, then one of the specially made cardboard transport cartons, available in pet shops for birds, gerbils, or guinea pigs, are adequate. If the journey will be longer, then you will need a small transport cage of 18½ by 6½ by 6½ inches (46 × 16 × 16 cm),

◀ Above: An eight-day-old chick at banding. Nestlings should be banded when they are between seven and ten days old. Below left: All nestlings among the Australian grassfinches strongly resemble each other. Only the mouth, palate, inside of the lower mandibles, and the tongue markings differ from species to species. The most noticeable markings consist of knobby papillae in the corners of the mouth. Below right: A one-year-old yellow-headed dilute-bodied male. This is a so-called body color mutation, which apparently occurs only in single factor males with a purple chest.

with a wire front only; all other sides being solid (sometimes referred to as a box cage). Such a cage is adequate for four to five birds; but not more! It must be furnished with a rough-textured perch, so that the birds have a good grip. I am convinced that such a small cage infinitely is better than a large cage and the birds will travel much more quietly, with less risk of the "panic moments" and consequences associated with large cages.

We must supply a small dish of seed of the type supplied by the vendor! The birds will be more at home with a seed mixture known to them. A few sprays of millet and a piece of water soaked bread or cake (to provide moisture if the birds are thirsty — a dish or hopper of water is likely to spill during the journey). As we know, Gouldians suck up their water, so as long as the bread or cake is soaked thoroughly there should be no problems. If transported in a car, the cage should be placed on the back seat and strapped in with the safety belt or similar. Protect from drafts and possible dangerous fumes. Never place the cage between your feet as you drive. Not only is that dangerous to yourself, it can be dangerous to the birds as they may be too near to the ventilator/heater. In cold weather — when tropical birds really should not be transported at all — we should warm up the car interior before introducing the cage. Gouldian finches cannot tolerate great or sudden changes in temperature.

The whole cage can be placed inside a grocery paper bag or can be wrapped like a parcel in brown paper (with ventilation holes of course). Don't stop too often. When transporting birds, take the quickest and most direct route home; it can only be best for the birds.

On arrival at home the birds should be placed, preferably separated, in roomy cages. Of course, the cages should have been prepared in advance, with water, food, and so on, and the temperature and humidity in the bird room should be correct. Birds that are destined for a garden aviary should first be kept under observation in an indoor cage for a week to ten days (see Acclimatizing New

Buying Gouldian Finches

Birds, following). When we know that our new birds are fit and healthy, we can then consider introducing them to their permanent homes.

Acclimatizing New Birds

As we have already discussed, newly acquired birds should be placed in separate cages, so that your existing stock is not infected with any disease accidentally brought in. Although the birds you purchase may have seemed perfectly well, there is no way of telling if they have something in the early stages. To be on the safe side, new birds are placed in a separate room, where there are no other birds and also where dogs, cats, and other pets cannot gain entry. The quarantine cages should *not* have sand covered perches or gravel on the floor—this could damage the feet and set off an infection. It is best to place grocery paper on the floor. Newspapers are unsuitable as the print can be unhealthy as well as soil the plumage.

Ensure that the situation in the quarantine room is extremely peaceful. Leave a night-light on for the first few nights so that the birds can find their way back to their rest-perches if, for one reason or other, they are disturbed. We must do all we can to reduce stress to its barest minimum, as stressed birds lose their resistances to various infectious disease organisms. This means that the drinking water should be sterilized by boiling and cooled before being offered. This should be given for at least the first four days. Personally, I prefer to give sterilized water for a week, to allay all risks of infection. The quarantine room should have the temperature maintained at 85°F (30°C) for at least a week. Thereafter, the temperature very gradually is reduced over another week to the optimum temperature required (see page 14).

For the first few days we must keep a close watch on the birds; especially to ensure that they can find their food. To allay possibilities of birds not using strange feeding containers, some seed should be strewn on the floor of the cage where the finches will be able to find it easily, until you are sure they are taking adequate seed from the hoppers. For safety's sake, place a shallow dish of water on the cage floor and change it several times a day. Such water should not be too cold, but preferably at room temperature (keep a covered bucket of fresh water in the room so that it reaches room temperature).

Stress

Stress is a condition in a bird (or any animal for that matter) that dramatically reduces the body's normal resistance to disease organisms. Body reserves are reduced and, it this occurs over an extended period, the bird will weaken drastically. Stress can be caused by various things, including capture (catching up), transport, strange surroundings, changes of food, changes (especially sudden) of temperature, inappropriate photoperiod (i.e. longer than 15 hours daylight each day), overcrowding, loud or long-lasting tumult, exhibitions, inoculations, diseases, breeding, molting, harassment by man or animal (dog, cat) and many more.

The symptoms can be subclinical, in that there are no obvious outward signs of particular diseases. In many cases, a bird may reduce its food consumption and be more susceptible to infection; it will start to waste and may suffer from diarrhea. Give a suitable tonic food (Universal-Plus or Avi-Start, both from L/M Animal Farms), which is easily digestible and eagerly accepted by the birds, and increase the concentrations of certain foodstuffs such as vitamin/mineral supplements, honey, millet spray, and so on.

Over the years it has become obvious that most birds suffer stress in the first few months of new ownership, and therefore are susceptible to all kinds of infections. The fancier must therefore do all he can to alleviate stress in his birds as much as possible.

Some recommendations to help you achieve this are:
• Buy *only* birds that are in prime health; if you are

unsure, get them inspected first by a more experienced fancier or by an avian veterinarian; there usually will be somebody in, or known by, your society who can assist. The vet could perform blood tests, although I think this should be avoided as far as possible with small birds such as Gouldians. In most cases a stool analysis can be adequate.

• Ensure that all new birds are quarantined separately from your existing stock (personally, I quarantine them for one month, to be on the safe side). Transmission of disease either way will thus be avoided.

• New arrivals must have peace and quiet, with disturbance at the absolute minimum.

• Maintain the optimum temperature (see p. 14) and humidity. If necessary a small portable heater can be used — this should not be too expensive.

• Ensure that the birds are not affected by drafts; one of our birds greatest enemies. To test for drafts, stand a burning candle near the cage; the slightest flicker of the flame will tell you that there is a draft. Move the cage until you find a draft-free spot or, find the source of the draft and stop it.

• New arrivals should be given the same type of food they are accustomed to even if it is not "by the book." Changes in the diet should be very gradual over a period of 10–14 days. Do not give grit in the first two weeks; birds suffering from stress have a tendency to swallow too much grit, with a danger of gut blockages and their consequences.

• New arrivals (and, in fact all of your birds) must have 12–15 hours rest each night. If you have birds in cages in the house, these should be covered with a thick towel or similar in the evening hours to block out as much light as possible. Try to keep the noise down.

• Although the birds in quarantine must be left in peace as much as possible; they should, of course, be quietly and carefully inspected each day — from a distance. Ensure that the birds remain healthy, look fit, have no puffed out feathers, are not over or underactive, are not over or under feeding. Do not smoke near your birds and keep noisy children and pets well away from them. Consult your avian veterinarian at the first sign of any sickness.

• New arivals frequently are suffering from overgrown nails. This can be a danger; they can get caught in the cage wire and may find it difficult to sit on the perch (without sand paper cover!). Nails can be clipped quite easily if you know what to do (see page 54).

Basic Rules for Housing

The Proper Environment

Fanciers wishing to fully appreciate their Gouldian finches must put a lot of consideration into how they are going to accommodate the birds. *Roomy* cages and aviaries, free of damp and drafts, are absolutely essential. As Gouldian finches, in contrast to many other finch species, are very dependent on warmth, it is not possible for many fanciers to keep their Gouldians in outdoor aviaries throughout the year; the answer therefore is indoor aviaries. Anyone wishing to take up intensive breeding of the birds will find a bird room with box or breeding cages the most effective solution.

Gouldian finches are extremely sensitive to changes. Once placed in position, perches, food and water vessels, bath containers, and so on should not be moved continually into different positions otherwise one will create unnecessary disquiet amongst the birds. The same goes for the general husbandry: try to maintain a fairly strict routine in feeding and cleaning of the cages, aviaries, and utensils. Do not move birds from one cage to another unless this is absolutely necessary; catching them in the hand already can cause a stressful situation! When you go in your bird room or aviaries, try to wear similar clothes all the time (many fanciers wear a dust coat), and signal your approach by saying something quietly or by whistling. In a short time the birds will then become accustomed to you and will even know when to expect a visit from you.

Temperature

It does not matter how good the housing for Gouldian finches is, it will not help if we do not maintain the correct temperatures. The same goes for humidity and light; there are thus three essential points to be considered for the successful maintenance of Gouldians.

The first factor, temperature, is extremely important: *Gouldian Finches must be kept at a minimum temperature of 70 to 77°F (21–25°C)*

In the wild, Gouldians live at even higher temperatures (see page 56). However the temperatures given here are a good average for our semi-domestic birds, providing this is maintained day *and* night. I would recommend a day temperature of 73 to 77°F (23–25°C), especially during the breeding season. It should never fall below the minimum temperature of 70°F (21°C). During the molt, even higher temperatures are recommended, preferably in the range of 81 to 84°F (27–29°C). A maximum and minimum thermometer is a very necessary instrument.

Humidity

Without adequate humidity, the breeding season will be, or almost be, a complete failure and it will be difficult for older birds to remain in good condition especially with regard to the plumage.

The humidity must be kept at a minimum of 55 to 60 percent and the means of raising it higher must be available.

At a temperature of 70 to 77°F (21–25°C), the humidity should be 55 to 65 percent minimum; higher temperatures, 65 to 70 percent. A good humidifier is thus essential.

Light

Cages and aviaries must be situated in a light, draft-free position, where natural sunlight will shine in daily.

It is not always possible to accomplish this. Therefore Vita Light (see page 54) with an automatic timer should be used. Naturally, bird rooms with a southerly or southwesterly aspect will ease the situation somewhat. Ensure also that the bird room does not become overheated in the summer, or lose heat too quickly in the winter. It is advisable to have a 7 watt night-light burning during the hours of darkness, so that birds shocked for one reason or another do not panic and injure themselves, and can find their way back to their perches.

Basic Rules for Housing

The Bird Room

For breeding Gouldian finches, a bird room is most suitable. You can have some indoor aviaries but, more important, a number of breeding (box) cages. Breeding cages are used so that individual pairs of birds can be controlled. Each pair gets its own breeding cage and several cages can be placed above each other. Ensure that the bottom cage is raised well from the floor. Not only will this make it easier for you to service, it will make it more difficult for vermin to interfere with the cages. One part of the bird room should be reserved for storage; utensils, medicines, and so on can be stored on a set of shelves. Seed should be stored in preferably metal or strong plastic containers with a good fitting lid. A large sink with a hot and cold water supply would be an ideal facility, whereas a work bench or table would be practical. A chair or two will allow you to sit and observe your birds peacefully.

Aviaries

Aviaries may be purchased in prefabricated form, erected by a contractor, or designed and built on your own. Quite often the latter is the most ideal for the person and situation in question. There are books available that deal exclusively with aviary building.

The Room Aviary

A room aviary often is confused with a bird room. However the bird room consists of an entire room with fixed or movable aviaries, cages, and so on and used wholly for birds, whereas the room aviary is just an aviary located in a room. In recent years, the room aviary has grown very popular and there are several attractive commercial models available. Some even have a set of wheels so that they easily can be pushed from one location to another — even outside in suitable weather. I have seen some lovely room aviaries in which breeding has been accomplished, even though children played nearby.

The Breeding or Box Cage

Small nervous birds like Gouldians always feel safer and thus more at ease in a cage that is enclosed from several sides. A box cage with solid top, bottom, sides, and back, and wire in the front only is the best as, to the bird, "danger" can only approach from one direction. Such a cage should be placed in a light location, but definitely not in full sun as the cage would soon turn into a veritable oven! Box cages especially are useful for the breeding of Gouldian finches (see page 31).

Personal Hygiene and Cleanliness

Various pathogenic (disease causing) organisms (protozoa, bacteria, viruses) can be transmit-

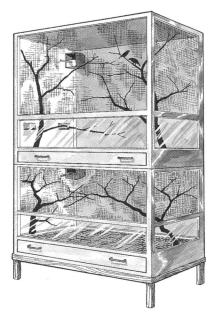

Breeding cages.

Basic Rules for Housing

ted from animal to man and vice versa. Adequate hygienic practices in our bird keeping' are extremely important to the health of both the birds *and* ourselves. Before handling any bird, the hands should be washed thoroughly — and washed again afterwards. This is important particularly if handling a sick or potentially sick bird — wash hands between handling each and every bird. The same goes for cleaning chores; always wash hands before starting on the next cage. If you have an outbreak of a serious disease in your bird room or aviaries, then rubber gloves should be worn; these must likewise be washed, disinfected, or changed from one job to the next.

Special attention must be given to feeding, drinking, and bathing containers that should be cleaned and disinfected daily. The plastic, galva-nized, or aluminum removable cage trays are cleaned similarly, at least every third day. (A layer of sand can be used as a tray covering, or a few sheets of newspaper laid on top of each other; the upper sheet can then be removed as it is soiled, thus disturbing the birds less often).

The floor of the bird room — which is best made of concrete covered with ceramic tiles or linoleum — should be cleaned and disinfected thoroughly every week. I personally use the product Lysol at the rate of 4 ounces per gallon of water.

Rats and mice, the bane of every aviculturist, also must be discouraged. There are various methods of control available; your local garden center or pet shop proprietor will be able to advise you on effective methods.

Foods and Feeding

All animals require a balanced diet and whether you are an elephant, an ant, a human being, or a Gouldian finch, you require six fundamental dietary constituents to ensure your diet is balanced. Various animals acquire their proteins, carbohydrates, fats, vitamins, minerals, and water in different ways and from different sources but the functions of these dietary constituents are basically the same in all species. Before working out a balanced diet for our Gouldians, let us take a brief look at each of these fundamental elements and discuss their functions.

Proteins

The actual body tissue of all animals is composed largely of various kinds of protein, each body being made up of countless cells. Each cell consists of a harder wall containing protoplasm, which itself is composed chiefly of proteins and water. All parts of a bird: the feathers, skin, feet, beak, muscles, internal organs (such as heart and liver), and of course eggs, are rich in protein. Proteins are essential for the growth, maintenance, and repair of all body tissues. Additionally, proteins are important for the correct functions of the organs and play a major role in the reproductive process.

Proteins are divided into two main categories: animal and vegetable (sometimes referred to as class I and class II). In general, animal proteins have a greater immediate, nutritive value than plant proteins (plant eating animals must convert the plant protein to animal protein before it can be used in the tissues). Sources of animal protein include meat, fish, eggs, and milk.

Throughout the year, a little stale brown bread soaked in water is an excellent dietary supplement for Gouldian finches, more so in the breeding season. Once accustomed to it, the birds will not only devour it enthusiastically, they will also feed it readily to their offspring. Water soaked brown bread should only be provided in the mornings and what is left over at midday should be removed and discarded.

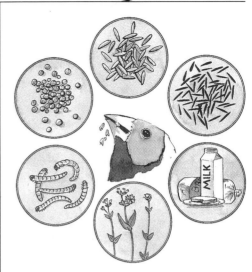

Gouldian finches require (clock wise, from the top): canary grass seed; niger seed; bread soaked in low-fat milk or water; greens, such as chickweed; insects, such as small mealworms; and various millets.

Proteins also can be fed to birds in the form of insects or commercially available protein concentrate (often called universal food or rearing food).

Gouldians obtain most of their plant protein from the great variety of seeds and green foods that should be offered to them. Chickweed and lettuce seem to be a great favorite (lettuce and other greens should be washed thoroughly under running cold water, to remove any impurities, then dried before being given to the birds). The major constituent of green food is water and as the water content is so high there is little room left for proteins. In fact the average content of protein in green food wavers only somewhere between 1.5 and 4.5 percent! Young, succulent shoots often are richer in protein than the full-grown leaves. Sprouting seeds and the young leaves of spinach and lettuce, for example, are much more nutritious than older leaves.

Foods and Feeding

Green food gradually will lose much of its nutritive value as summer wears on, unless you plant small quantities of seed at regular intervals; thus ensuring a regular supply of young growth. Remember, however, that ripe seed has a greater protein content than unripe seed.

Feathers, beak, and claws are composed chiefly of keratin, which itself is a form of protein. It is therefore essential that nestlings and fledglings, during their main period of growth, receive an adequate supply of protein-rich food. A protein deficiency at this important time will have a drastic effect on the development of the youngsters. A protein deficiency also will reduce the nutritional value of other dietary constituents. Some difficulties experienced by bird breeders, even cannibalism, can be related to a dietary deficiency of protein. (Of course, protein deficiency is not always the cause of these problems, but it always should be taken into account.)

As the various sources of protein are composed differently, it is important to offer a variety. Even foodstuffs that are apparently the same can vary in composition, depending on where they were grown and how they were cultivated. For example, it is estimated that the protein content of a good standard seed mixture for finches could vary between 12 and 16 percent.

Remember that protein can only be utilized efficiently in the body if it is accompanied by an adequate intake of vitamins and minerals. Remember also that most insects have a hard chitinous exoskeleton that, although composed chiefly of protein, is barely digestible. Try, therefore, to feed your birds those softer kinds of insects (and other invertebrates) such as mealworms, enchytrae (whiteworms), flies, and their larvae, rather than beetles, ants and such.

Carbohydrates

Carbohydrates are produced by plants in the presence of sunlight by a process known as photosynthesis. By combining the elements carbon, hydrogen, and oxygen (taken from the air and water), simple sugars, or monosaccharides ($C_6 H_{12} O_6$) are produced by the plants; further complicated processes produce the more complex di-, tri-, and polysaccharides. Glucose and fructose are common monosaccharides; refined cane sugar, or sucrose ($C_{12} H_{22} O_{11}$) is a disaccharide; starch is a polysaccharide.

Carbohydrates are the primary source of energy. They are necessary to keep the body warm and to provide fuel for muscular activity (flying, for example). Too much carbohydrate from grain foods can be bad for your finch's plumage.

Fats and Oils

A bird may obtain fat from two primary sources: directly from the oil contained in many seeds and indirectly by converting excess dietary carbohydrate into fat within the body. These two sources generally are adequate for the needs of most cage or aviary birds, though the addition of a few drops of fish liver oil to the birds' seed (about two drops to 1 pound (.5 kg) of seed) may help. Remember however, that too much fat in the diet can be as harmful as too little. Birds that become too fat rarely are good breeders and they are likely to have problems with the molt. This problem occasionally may arise in cage birds that get too little exercise or that receive excessive oil or carbohydrate containing seeds.

Vitamins

Whereas proteins, carbohydrates, and fats are required by all animals in relatively large quantities and often are referred to collectively as "macronutrients," vitamins and minerals are required in much smaller quantities and often are called "micronutrients." This does not mean, however, that the micronutrients are any less important. For example, a deficiency of any one important vitamin can result in severe disability and can be even life-threatening. Without certain vitamins, life it-

Foods and Feeding

self virtually is impossible. In spite of this, we only began to understand the importance of them as recently as 1912.

Vitamins can be divided broadly into two groups: those that are fat-soluble and those that are water-soluble. In the former category we find vitamins A, D, E, and K, whereas vitamin C and those of the B-complex are found in the latter.

Fat-Soluble Vitamins

Vitamin A (Retinol): This vitamin is fundamental to the metabolism of body cells, the maintenance of skin and mucous membranes, and the enhancement of sight. It also has a influence on the function of the respiratory system and plays a part in the pigmentation of the retina, thus allowing the eye to function in poor light.

Foods that contain vitamin A in useful quantities and that you can give to your birds include egg yolk, fresh greens (especially finely chopped chickweed, spinach, lettuce, and dandelion). Greens and various roots (especially carrots) contain carotene, from which vitamin A can be manufactured. In general, seeds are low in vitamin A content but various millets may contain significant amounts. By far the best source of vitamin A is cod-liver oil.

During the breeding season, birds require a much greater supply of vitamin A than normal. Although they will not necessarily become sterile with a deficiency of the vitamin, they will be likely to have all sorts of brooding problems and the resulting youngsters may be weak and unhealthy.

Vitamin A is sometimes called the anti-infection or growth vitamin; also the anti-sterility or fertility vitamin, a name sometimes mistakenly given to vitamin D (see next section). Various supplementary vitamin A/D preparations are available commercially and may be found under a number of trade names. Excessive vitamins are disposed of in the liver but be aware that an overdose of vitamin A can result in a fading of the plumage, whereas too much D can cause decalcification of the bones.

Vitamin D3 (Cholecalciferol): Sometimes known as the sunshine vitamin or sometimes as the anti-rickets vitamin, vitamin D is found primarily in fish oils, followed by egg yolk and milk. One of the best ways of ensuring that your birds receive enough vitamin D is to give them access to sunshine, which activates the provitamins in the birds' skin.

Birds kept in outdoor aviaries with adequate unfiltered sunlight normally do not require supplementary vitamin D except in the breeding season, though birds kept indoors or away from sunshine should receive supplements of liver oil or a commercial vitamin A/D supplement.

Vitamin E (Tocopherol): Like vitamin A, this is also often called the anti-sterility or fertility vitamin. However its function is not so much concerned with fertility as with the normal growth and development of the embryo and hatchling. Adequate quantities of vitamin E are to be found naturally in germinated seeds, whereas wheat germ oil or corn germ oil are excellent supplementary sources. The edible green leaves of many plants including chickweed, watercress, spinach, kale, lettuce, and so on are also a good source of vitamin E.

Vitamin E is important for the development of the nerve cells of the brain, the skeletal muscles, the protein content of the blood, the correct function of the sperm-producing parts of the testes and especially for the overall growth and development of the embryo. It obviously should never be absent from a bird's diet and should be given in the form of germinated seed or with supplementary wheat germ.

Vitamin K: Primarily known as the blood-clotting vitamin, vitamin K (K is from the Danish *Koagulation*), or a lack of it, poses no problems to birds receiving a varied diet. Green food, carrot tops, kale, alfalfa, and some grains have a high vitamin K content. Unlike most other vitamins, vitamin K is not destroyed by heating.

Foods and Feeding

Water-Soluble Vitamins

At the present time there are some 14 recognized components of the vitamin B-complex and there is a good chance that more will be discovered in the future. These vitamins are essential to all animals including our Gouldian finches and, fortunately, are contained in substantial quantities in the seeds that form the staple part of our birds' diet.

Vitamin B1 (Thiamine): A severe deficiency of this vitamin causes beriberi in humans, but its general function is to aid the steady and continuous release of energy from the carbohydrates in the diet. A deficiency can cause a check in the normal growth of embryo and hatchling. Good sources of thiamine are in the germ cells of grain seeds and legumes and in yeast preparations, whereas smaller amounts occur in meat, powdered milk, eggs, fruit, and green food. Although present in the seed husk, it is not used efficiently by our birds unless they get very young, unripe seed as part of their diet.

Vitamin B2 or G (Riboflavin): Another vitamin associated with growth, riboflavin is found mainly in yeast, but green leaves, powdered milk, and eggs are also good sources. Adequate quantities of this vitamin occur in the germ of good quality seeds and these, coupled with a regular supply of green food will prevent any deficiency. A shortage of riboflavin in the diet can cause inefficient egg production, deaths in the shell, inflammation of the feet, twisted toes, poor down and feather development, poor growth, inflamed skin, and other problems.

Choline: A deficiency of this vitamin, in association with a shortage of manganese, leads to a fatty liver, a problem that, in the poultry industry, is referred to as "perosis." Choline is found largely in the linings of the intestines where it plays a part in the maintenance of peristalsis. It also regulates the transport of fatty acids and the breaking down of them in the liver. In general, a deficiency will cause inflammation and swelling in the joints in developing nestlings; the birds are unable to hold themselves in a normal position and malformed growth will be the result. Another result of deficiency is internal disturbances in breeding hens, leading to the laying of few and poor eggs. In order to avoid deficiencies of this and other vitamins, ensure that seed of only the highest quality is given and leave out soft food that contains few vitamins. Rich sources of choline include brewer's yeast, fishmeal, and grains.

Biotin: Probably one of the most important vitamins of the B group, biotin is sometimes referred to as vitamin H. A deficiency of the vitamin can result in severe skin and plumage problems. Although relatively large amounts of biotin occur in eggs yolks, raw egg whites contain a substance that destroys it when they are mixed together. This action can be prevented, however, if the eggs are boiled whole and mashed together *after* cooking. The vitamin also occurs in cow's milk, yeast, carrots, and spinach. Fresh seeds contain adequate amounts of biotin but of course the quantity will vary between types and quality.

Vitamin B12 (Cyanocobalamine or Cobalamine): Containing traces of the elements cobalt and phosphorus, this vitamin stimulates the growth, particularly of the plumage. It also plays a part in the creation of blood, in the formulation of methionine from cystine, and in the synthesis of proteins. It is most abundant in fishmeal and other animal products, yeast, and milk products. B12 also can be manufactured and stored in crystalline form. However do not add it to the food as the quantity must be regulated scientifically to prevent an overdose.

Vitamin C (Ascorbic Acid): Everyone knows how essential vitamin C is to us humans. Gouldian finches and other birds also require the vitamin but, unlike us, they can manufacture the vitamin synthetically during the process of digestion. It therefore is unnecessary to give our Gouldians a supplement of vitamin C except in special circumstances, such as when a bird is afflicted by disease or poisoning, or to fortify it against stress when in a traveling cage or being exhibited. Vitamin C cannot be stored in the body, so any excess is soon lost.

Minerals

Like vitamins, certain minerals are extremely important micronutrients in the diets of all animals. The most important mineral of all is calcium (Ca), without which, for example, it would be impossible for our hen birds to form eggs. Some of the other minerals that must not be absent from a bird's diet include phosphorus (P), sodium (Na), chlorine (Cl), potassium (K), magnesium (Mg), iron (Fe), zinc (Zn), copper (Cu), sulphur (S), iodine (I), and manganese (Mn).

Calcium and Phosphorus

These two elements usually are included together when nutrition is discussed as they are very closely interrelated in the way they function in the body. Calcium is indispensable in the manufacture and maintenance of the skeleton, in the coagulation of the blood, in the correct functioning of the sinews and organs such as the heart, and in the formation of eggshell. Phosphorus also is important in the formation and maintenance of the skeletal structure, in addition to playing an important function in body metabolism; it also may be a constituent of certain proteins or fats. In the wild, birds keep themselves very healthy by foraging around for extra mineral-containing items as they feed. The ratio of calcium to phosphorus in the diet is important for both elements to be used efficiently. Birds require about three times as much calcium as phosphorus and it is very important that this balance is maintained, or the bodily functions will, sometimes very seriously, be disturbed. For your captive Gouldians, you should not need to worry as phosphorus is contained in sufficient quantities in green foods and seeds you offer them. However, adequate calcium usually is not available unless you provide your Gouldians

with the appropriate supplements. Good sources of additional calcium include dicalcium phosphate, chalk (rock chalk, *not* blackboard chalk), cuttle bone, grit (especially oyster grit), crushed eggshells (sterilized), and pulverized limestone.

Other Minerals

Experiments have shown that small amounts of magnesium containing salts in a bird's diet help it to maintain the correct balance of calcium, phosphorus, and vitamin D and, with calcium, is necessary for bone formation. A deficiency of magnesium will lead to convulsions, stunted growth, poor bone structure, and sparse feathering. An adequate supply of magnesium is contained in good quality seeds.

Gouldian finches also require iodine, copper, and many other minerals, mostly in minute quantities. Most of these essential minerals are contained (as salts or compounds) in the normal foodstuffs, including seeds and green food. Small amounts of iodine are contained in cuttle bone, seashell grit, oyster shells, meat, milk, and eggs. Fishmeal and cod-liver oil are rich in iodine but wheat germ oil is not. With our recommended regular feeding with stale brown bread soaked in water, your birds should never experience an iodine deficiency (which causes goiter).

Copper is necessary for the efficient manufacture of blood and hemoglobin; it also activates the absorption of iron into the system (via the intestines). A shortage of copper results in anemia.

Iron and manganese in the red blood cells bind the oxygen from the air taken into the lungs and promote a good circulation. Sulphur and silicon help in the formation of the plumage and add to its luster.

Potassium, sodium, and iron are useful in controlling the incidence of certain parasites. Sodium also helps in the coordination of tissue construction and neutralizes carbon dioxide as well as assists in the assimilation of food.

Foods and Feeding

Insoluble Grit

As well as soluble grits, which contain many essential elements and are broken down quickly in the gut, a good supply of insoluble grit also is important as it assists the gizzard muscles in grinding up food such as seed. Various grit mixtures are available from your suppliers; these include sea sand and ground granite, which are insoluble in the stomach and act as grindstones until they are worn small enough to pass through the system.

Water

Birds can go without food for longer than they can go without water; some birds are unable to survive more than 24 hours without this "elixir of life." Grassfinches, including Gouldians, have relatively greater tolerances for drought (reflect-

Check at least twice a day to make sure the water supply is in order, more often during hot summer weather. To give your birds a special treat, dissolve some honey or grape sugar (glucose) in the drinking water several times per week. Gouldian Finches suck water by means of peristaltic movements of the esophagus (see page 61).

ing upon the wild habitats) but this does not mean that they ever should be denied a permanent supply of fresh water.

As well as forming by far the greatest part of the living body, water is essential for the transport of food through the digestive system; it softens the food in the crop and acts as a solvent for the enzymes that digest the food. It acts as a structural element in the cells and helps regulate the body temperature. This latter function is very important as birds do not have sweat glands, so the excess warmth must be expelled via lungs and air sacs. An overheated bird also will fluff out its feathers to allow cool air between them.

Green Foods

Ideally, our green food should come from a number of different sources. Unfortunately, most of us who live in the cities and urban areas have to obtain our supplies from the local supermarket. However, most people have the possibility of growing at least some of their own green food, even if it is in pots and tubs on the balcony or even on a sunny window ledge.

You can buy special seed mixtures from your pet shop or avicultural supplier. A large plant trough or a number of tubs and pots will enable you to grow enough green food for the whole year. Chickweed, a great favorite with many birds, is easy to grow. Certain bird seeds allowed to germinate also are good (millet and niger seed germinate very quickly), especially when young are being reared.

Do not immerse the seeds in water when germinating them or they will lose much of their nourishment. Keep them just moist. One way of doing this is to place the seed in a kitchen sieve, run water through it, then spread the seed out on damp tea towels or paper towels. The moment the seeds begin to germinate (after three or four days), they are washed in cold water, then given to the birds. It is not necessary to wait until the seed sprouts.

Foods and Feeding

All green foods should be washed thoroughly under a running tap and the water shaken out before being fed to the birds. This will not remove all dangers by any means but at least we will have done our best. Avoid collecting wild green foods near roads as vehicular exhausts can pollute them with toxic substances. Never give green food that has wilted, or that which likely is to be polluted by chemical sprays (insecticides, fungicides, herbicides) or the urine and droppings of wild or domestic animals. Green food should be given fresh, every day, but only in small quantities. I personally do not give my birds more food than they comfortably can devour in a few hours. Nor do I ever give green food late in the day. Gouldians should fill their crops with solid (seed) food before retiring for the night.

Chickweed, *Stellaria media,* is one of the most nutritious kinds of green food and is very common as a weed in most gardens. It also is easy to grow. Birds will eat the leaves and seed. I have yet to encounter a breeder who had a bad word for chickweed. Many give it to their birds in virtually unlimited quantities, but, personally, I oppose this as too much of it can cause diarrhea. I also use lettuce, spinach, and similar vegetables very sparingly. Lettuce is a particularly laxative plant if eaten in too large amounts.

Spinach is rich in vitamins and iron and is beneficial particularly if given together with another green food or seed rich in calcium. Watercress, poppy seed, and sesame seed are excellent in this respect. Watercress also is rich in iron. Another green food rich in vitamins is the green top of the carrot. A great favorite is the dandelion *(Taraxacum officinale)*; both the flowers and leaves are eaten greedily by the birds especially if they are hung up in bunches. In fact, all parts of the dandelion; leaves, flowers, stalks, and roots, may be offered safely. Dandelions contain a high proportion of vitamin A as does parsley, shepherd's purse, red and white clover, cabbage leaves (the darker the leaves the better), Brussels sprouts, and celery. It is pointless using the white parts of let-

Gouldian finches cannot be kept in top condition on a diet of seed only. They also require greens, especially in the breeding season. From left to right: shepherd's purse, dandelion, watercress, and chickweed.

tuce and celery as they possess virtually no nutritive value. While growing, all green food contains a relatively high percentage of protein and carotene; mature leaves contain much less protein.

Seeds

The most important kinds of seeds for Gouldians include canary grass seed, white millet, panicum millet, plate millet, Japanese millet, millet spray (which should always be available; the birds will spend hours busy in a bunch of millet sprays hung up in a corner of the cage or aviary), and niger seed although this often is not so popular.

Over the years, it has been ascertained that white millet is *not* poisonous, in spite of statements in the thirties to the contrary by the well-known Gouldian breeder, P.W. Teague. The means by which seed is given raises arguments among many fanciers. Many like to mix the seed varieties together, but others like to give each kind of seed in separate earthenware dishes.

23

Foods and Feeding

My personal experience is that my birds feed better if given a choice of seeds separately, than if given a seed mixture. However, in addition to seeds in separate dishes, I also give them a commercial mixture. This gives the birds ''entertainment,'' and I have noticed often that they may take occasional seeds of a different kind to those listed above. This is good of course; there certainly is nothing wrong with a change now and again!

Some examples of seed mixtures are:

I	
Canary grass seed	30 percent
Panicum millet	25 percent
White millet	25 percent
Plate millet	20 percent

II	
Canary grass seed	25 percent
White millet	20 percent
Panicum millet	20 percent
Plate millet	20 percent
Japanese millet	10 percent
Niger seed	5 percent

Germinated Seeds

As we have seen on page 22, germinated seeds are extremely good for Gouldian finches and should never be absent from their diet. Such seeds are valuable especially in the breeding season, and a daily supply of germinated grass and weed seeds should be available to the birds. Germinated seeds in the diet make a supply of green food less important (but green food still is to be recommended). Germinated seeds are rich in vitamin A and the enzyme catalase (an enzyme used in the blood to bring about the breakdown of hydrogen peroxide into water and oxygen). Although the process of germination uses up a portion of the carbohydrate content, the protein content is increased proportionately.

To germinate the seeds, first wash them under running, clean, cold water (an ordinary kitchen strainer is ideal for this). Then place them on a dry towel and pat out most of the moisture. The seeds are then spread out on damp paper towels or burlap sacking laid in plastic, glass, stainless steel, or chromium plated trays (not galvanized containers as chemical reactions with the zinc could affect the seed; if you really do not have any alternative, you must first paint the interior of the container with a good, lead-free paint. A regular control is necessary and each container should be repainted when necessary). The same goes for the containers in which the germinated seeds are given to the birds and all containers must be scrubbed and scalded under boiling water (and allowed to cool) before each use.

The germinating seeds should be spread out as evenly as possible and should not lay in heaps. Each seed should be in contact with the damp towel or sacking and also should have air circulating around it. If using old sacking, it must first be boiled to kill off any possible disease organisms.

Germinating seed must not be immersed in water, which causes them to lose much of their nutritive value. Instead, the seed should be kept just moist. Personally, I have always had good success washing seed in a kitchen sieve, then placing it over a bucket. Pour water over the seeds daily. In about three to four days the sprouted seeds will be ready for feeding to your finches.

Foods and Feeding

The seeds can be kept just moist (definitely *not* wet) by using a houseplant watering device (if artificial fertilizer has been used in it, give it a thorough cleaning first). The container is placed in a light, well-ventilated spot, out of any extremes of temperature. The best germination temperatures usually are in the range of 77 to 85°F (25-30°C).

Seeds for Gouldian Finches

Wild birds are their own masters and fulfill their own nutritional requirements. They are very clever at doing this and have learned to do so over millions of years of inherited evolutionary experience and instinct. Most wild birds are in excellent health, and nutritional disturbances may occur only in times of acute climatic disasters.

In captivity, birds are unable to be their own nutritional masters and must make do with what they are given. It is therefore important that we understand that our birds receive a balanced diet, accomplished with a *variety* of seeds and green foods. It is understandable that commercial birdseed mixtures with their fixed percentages of various seeds are not always the answer to satisfying your birds' needs. I am a great believer in the use of various kinds of seeds given separately in automatic seed dispensers, which are available in various models from avicultural suppliers. It is then easy to monitor which kinds of seeds are eaten in preference to others. Three or four such dispensers will be well worth the money as seed wastage will be eliminated. It is possible to make your own seed dispensers but do not use plywood as, after a time, the sheets will separate, forming ideal hiding places for unpleasant organisms.

One disadvantage of automatic seed dispensers is that they may become blocked from time to time. Regular checks therefore are essential. The dispensers should be placed in the covered part of the aviary or in a light part of the night shelter. It is a good idea to provide some extra food hoppers, perhaps two in the covered flight, and one in the

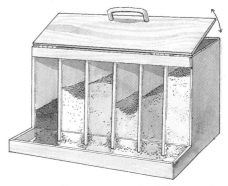

A hopper with compartments for different seeds. See text on page 24.

night shelter. To have to squabble or fight over food containers can be very stressful to a group of birds, particularly the weaker members of the group that may go short of food. In any case, ensure that the birds you keep together in groups are all compatible with each other and keep an eye on them (but do not assume automatically that a resting bird is being kept away from the food). Remember that each bird is an individual and does not always conform to everything you may read in books; this is a good thing however, as it makes your hobby all the more interesting.

Starchy Seeds

Canary grass seed or White seed *(Phalaris canariensis)*: one of the best known birds seeds, Canary grass is eaten greedily and in large amounts by Gouldian finches. The quality is very variable depending on where it is cultivated; the best probably is Mazagan grass seed, which, together with Spanish seed, is most often used in seed mixtures. The seed cultivated in Argentina, Australia, Morocco, and Turkey is somewhat inferior. Spanish grass seed is the largest in size. Canary seed is very high in carbohydrate (66 percent) but fat (7 percent) is relatively low. The protein content of the seed is about 14 percent; the

Foods and Feeding

lysine content is low and cystine is lacking altogether.

Millet seed (*Panicum spp* and *Setaria spp*): These small, spherical seeds form the bulk of most seed mixtures. There are several kinds that are more or less similar in appearance; most are very poor in lycine but rich in leucine. Many fanciers grow their own white millet *(Panicum miliaceum),* which does well in poor soil and with little rain. The plants may reach 12 feet (3.7 m) in height! The "real" millet sprays *(Setaria viride)* are available in pet stores. These always should be available in the cage or aviary; Gouldians are crazy about them! The types of millet include: white, yellow, red, and Japanese. Senegal millet is very small grained, unlike Japanese, and thus is used often for small waxbills, but it is also a great favorite with Gouldians. Most millets contain about 60 percent carbohydrates, 12 percent proteins, 4 percent fat, and 4 percent minerals as well as essential amino acids in the form of lysine, methionine, tyrosine, and cystine in useful amounts.

Oily Seeds

Niger seed (*Guizota oleifera*): There are many kinds of oily or fatty seeds but Niger seed is probably the only one suitable for inclusion in the diet of our Gouldian finches. Niger seed is grown in many parts of the world for the production of vegetable oil but especially along the valley of the river Niger in Africa, where there are many plantations. Niger seeds are very beneficial to Gouldians during the colder parts of the year, but they also should be available to hens in the spring prior to the breeding season. Many fanciers withdraw the ration of niger seed after laying is completed.

Niger seeds are high in protein (about 21 percent) and extremely high in oil (fat) (about 40 percent). Carbohydrate at about 13 percent also is represented amply. They contain almost 4 percent minerals, including relatively high amounts of calcium and potassium; additionally, essential amino acids including lysine, cystine, tyrosene, and methionine make this an altogether very useful addition to the diet. However, it should not form more than 5 percent of the total diet and it only should be purchased in small amounts at a time as its high fat content renders it quickly rancid if damaged or spoiled.

Rearing Food

The majority of seedeating birds hatch from the egg in a relatively early stage of development. It must be obvious that during this time of growth and development, it is essential that the hatchlings receive a rich and diverse supply of food.

Wild seedeating birds, including Gouldians, will forage for large numbers of insects, as well as seeds, leaves, and grasses to ensure that their youngsters receive a varied diet, often much more so than possible in captivity. Luckily, there are a number of rearing diets available that provide an adequate substitute for the varied wild diet, especially for the canary and finch breeder. It is a fact that similar amounts of amino acids, fats, carbohydrates, vitamins, and minerals are required by all young birds, and, therefore, rearing foods that contain these essential ingredients should produce healthy youngsters. However, it is an unfortunate fact that many of these rearing foods contain by-products that are not necessarily accepted by all birds. It is thus advisable to provide your birds initially with a choice of two or three sorts of rearing food so that the parent birds can themselves decide what is best for their nestlings. In my own experience, I have achieved the best results with

Left, a yellow or orange-headed Gouldian. (Often ▶ referred to as *Chloebia gouldiae armitiana*, this variety is extremely scarce in the wild, representing less than 0.005% of the population. Although not rare in captivity, it is less abundant in domestic collections than the two other varieties.) Right, in the recessive white-breasted yellow mutation, the original chest color is eliminated, resulting in a white chest.

the following: Cédé-eivoer, a product of Holland that is available in the United States and Great Britain in the better pet shops, and two American products: Avi-Start and Universal-Plus, both obtainable from L/M Animal Farms (Pleasant Plain, Ohio 45162), and also available in most pet shops.

Insects

Many so-called seedeating birds include varying amounts (sometimes quite high percentages) of insects in their diets. Gouldians are no exception and will use insects especially when they are rearing their young; thus ensuring that the nestlings receive important animal protein to help them in their critical growing period. Professor Dr. Karl Immelmann, a German orinthologist, stated that Gouldian finches in the wild probably included more spiders and insects (flying termites, flies, flying ants, beetles, and so on) in their diet than most other Australian grass finches. In fact, he observed that they become completely insectivorous during the breeding season.

Suitable insect (and other invertebrate) foods for captive Gouldians include ants' "eggs" (really pupae), spiders, flies, tubifex, waterfleas, small mealworms, whiteworms *(Enchytraeus),* crickets, grasshoppers, beetles, fruit flies, maggots, and wax moths. Specialist companies supply cultures of many suitable invertebrate foods with instructions on how to proliferate them. It is recommended that the Gouldian fancier make himself familiar with two or three invertebrate species and culture a ready supply for use in the breeding season.

◀ Above left: A yellow-headed white-breasted yellow Gouldian. Above right: A diluted yellow Gouldian. Below left: A red-headed Gouldian. In the literature this bird is often referred to as *Chloebia gouldiae mirabilis* Below right: A male orange-headed dilutedbacked Gouldian.

Food Requirements in the Life of a Gouldian Finch

• Adult, nonbreeding or nonmolting birds, require food that is rich in carbohydrates, as they are active birds using much energy. The growing process has come to a halt so that the intake of proteins, vitamins, and minerals is reduced.

• A chick, on the contrary, requires large amounts of proteins, vitamins, and minerals as these are essential for adequate growth. As a chick is less active than an adult (it sits in the nest, does not fly or walk, and does not need to forage for food) it requires less energy and thus relatively smaller amounts of carbohydrates.

• An adult bird in breeding condition requires a very well-balanced diet, in which all of the essential proteins, carbohydrates, fats, vitamins, and minerals are available in high percentages. For the hen, in particular, which must produce good eggs and healthy embryos, such a diet is essential.

• A molting bird also requires a high intake of protein and this is understandable when one considers that 90 percent of each feather consists of protein. In addition, there is a substantial increase (probably about 15 percent) in the metabolism of fats and carbohydrates in order to keep the body at its correct temperature during the molt.

• During the breeding season, in addition to a good seed mixture, grit, cuttle bone, vitamins and minerals, a good brand of rearing food, green food, and (especially) germinated seed should be given. The "menu" can be enriched further by supplying insects and weed seeds.

• Outside the breeding season, in addition to a good seed mixture, grit, and cuttle bone, the occasional vitamin/mineral supplement and green food should be given.

• It can happen sometimes that certain birds will not accept food that they do not recognize, even when it is an important part of the diet. As Gouldians are naturally curious birds, I place such food in open dishes on a stand about 2 feet (.6 m) high and they soon investigate. In extreme cases, remove their normal food for a few hours (not more!).

Cleanliness and Hygiene

One of the most important aspects of disease prevention is the application of hygienic practices with regard to foods and feeding. Feeding utensils should be cleaned daily. Empty the seeds from containers out onto a sheet of newspaper and wipe out the dish. Blow away the empty hulls from the seed, mix in some new seed, and refill the containers. By doing this, you eliminate the risk that the lower layer of seed in the dish could become progressively older, spoil and provide a breeding ground for disease organisms.

By getting into the habit of cleaning out the seed dishes daily, one can avoid the "beginner's mistake" of frequently topping up dishes with fresh seed on top of empty hulls, so that eventually the birds receive inadequate food.

In addition to a daily cleaning, all food and water dishes, utensils, and so on should be cleaned more thoroughly and disinfected at least once per week. Make sure that seed containers are bone dry before refilling with seed as moist seed will spoil quickly and pose a possible danger to your birds' health.

Breeding Gouldian Finches

In their native habitat, Gouldian finches reproduce mainly in the latter part of the wet season, when there is adequate drinking water and the grass is abundant with seeds. At this time, there also is a large variety of insects available; they are not only eaten with zest by the adults, but form a large part in the diet of the growing nestlings.

Breeding Condition — Essential for Success

In nature, the reproductive season is triggered by a change in the photoperiod (as the hours of daylight lengthen) coupled with the availability of food. Gouldian finches inhabit an area where they usually breed when adequate grass and seeds of other plants, as well as insects are available. This is the wet season. It is interesting to note here that captive Gouldians do not seem to be dependent on particular seasons for breeding as long as they have the necessary conditions; i.e., a well-balanced diet and the correct temperature and humidity. The food must be rich in protein, so a good rearing food, insects, and grass seeds, as well as suitable accommodation, are very important.

Most successful breeders use breeding cages situated indoors (see page 15), but prior to this the male and female birds usually are kept separately in roomy (outdoor) aviaries. It is recommended that, outside the breeding season, the birds have room to relax and exercise to their hearts' content. The youngsters stand a better chance of fully developing in an aviary, of coming well through the molt, and of becoming accustomed to a "captive life." At the beginning of autumn the birds are caught up carefully and placed in their respective breeding cages. (Fall is the time that I *personally* regard as the beginning of the breeding season and many are in agreement with me. However there is no reason why breeding cannot be carried out at any time of the year; although my best results have been in the fall.) If your birds are leg banded (and they should be if you are a serious breeder) there will be no problem in pairing up those from which you think you will get the best results. It would, of course, be ideal to have the breeding cages installed in a specially equipped bird room.

The bird room should be kept at a consistent temperature of 77°F (25° C) with a humidity of 70 percent. You should have a good thermometer and a hygrometer to monitor the environment.

It is highly recommended that the birds receive approximately 15 hours of light each day (use full spectrum fluorescent) which, in spite of the time of the year (autumn), naturally should not astonish us.

It is a well-known fact that certain birds in the wild and in captivity can become sexually mature in as little as four to five months of age. However, experience has shown us that this is too early for successful breeding. Personally, I believe pairs should be at least 10–12 months old before they are paired. This will help to avoid egg-binding, abandoning of eggs or hatchlings, and other unpleasant consequences.

Breeding in Cages

The combined experiences of several generations of Gouldian breeders have shown that greater success is expected when the birds are bred in breeding cages rather than outdoor aviaries. Breeding cages are fairly easy to construct, but if you do not consider yourself a handyperson, there are many ready-made models to choose from in the pet stores. I have been most successful with box cages (closed from all sides except for the wire front) measuring 40 by 20 by 20 inches (102 × 51 × 51 cm); of course a couple of inches either way won't make much difference.

Many breeders use banks of cages placed side by side or on top of each other. Adjacent cages may be attached together (with hooks and eyes, top and bottom) and separated by a sliding panel, which, if removed, gives a double length "flight" cage ideal for the youngsters to develop once they leave the nests. This is an ideal solution for those

Breeding Gouldian Finches

fanciers who may not have the facilities to possess a garden aviary. The inside of the breeding cages should be painted. I use light pastel blue or light pastel green vinyl silk emulsion, which is harmless to the birds, easy to clean, and enhances the colors of the birds beautifully.

Before being used at the beginning of the breeding season, breeding cages should be thoroughly cleaned and disinfected (use, for example, a Lysol dilution of 4 ounces per gallon of water). Allow to thoroughly dry out and repaint if necessary. The floor of the cage should be covered with a 1 inch (2.5 cm) layer of mini corn cob, in which 4–5 teaspoons of oyster shell grit and 2 teaspoons of crushed charcoal are mixed. A cuttle bone should be clipped to the inside of the cage front and you can also crush some cuttle bone up and mix it with the floor covering (3–4 teaspoons). The birds eagerly will seek out the nutritious "food" among the corn.

Two perches, from front to back, should be placed one at each end of the breeding cage. These should be of varying thicknesses (respectively ¼ inch [.5 cm] and ⅜ inch [1 cm] diameter). In order to facilitate pairing and rest, the perches should not be too smooth and should be slightly flattened on the upper side. One perch should be high, close to the roof of the cage — but not so close that a bird cannot sit upright; the other perch should be lower, about halfway up the height of the cage. (Do not place perches so close to the walls that the birds cannot turn without damaging their wing or tail feathers.) Perches affixed in this manner will give the birds maximum flying room in the breeding cage; good for the further development of the fledgling young as well as for exercising the brooding adults, and for the metabolism.

One or two nest boxes can be situated in the breeding cage (if you use two, offer different types so that the birds have a choice). The ideal size is 8 inches long by 6 inches high by 6 inches wide (20 × 15 × 15 cm). One box can be half open, the other with an entrance hole 2 inches (5 cm) in diameter. Install, *inside* the box, just below

the entrance hole, a little "step" or edge about 1 inch high by 2 inches wide (2.5 × 5 cm). The birds then will be able to make a comfortable nest in the rest of the box and the step will be used by the birds when they are feeding their young. It also will prevent eggs or young falling accidentally from the nest box.

Although nest boxes can be placed inside the cage (for example, in each corner against the rear wall), they also can be placed outside the cage, either on the wire front or on a side wall. This will leave more space inside for the birds and will make our inspections of the nest much easier. A nestbox *in* the cage is almost impossible to inspect without alarming the birds.

The disadvantages of a nest box situated outside the cage are that the birds are unable to sit on the roof of the box to "guard the nest." Also, birds often land on the roof of the box, before making a little bow, to gain entrance to the nest. We can help by placing a small perch about 4 inches (10 cm long,) just below the entrance to the nest box. This will help young Gouldians (especially inexperienced pairs that often take a week to "come to a decision") to choose a nest box. They can sit together on the little perch and peer with outstretched necks into the cavity.

An advantage of the nest box placed *inside* the cage is that a brooding bird will be prepared for a visit from its mate when it lands on the roof of the box. It will hear the pitter-patter of its feet first, before it makes its entrance. Without this, of course, the entrance will be more sudden and could frighten brooding birds or nestlings.

The nest boxes themselves should be made from solid, natural wood (not plywood, chipboard, or similar). Most books recommend a minimum size of 6 by 6 by 6 inches (15 × 15 × 15 cm), with a half open front side. I have had greater success with the larger size mentioned previously, with a 2 inch (5 cm) entrance hole. Such nest boxes are used by budgerigar breeders and are readily available from avicultural suppliers. Do-it-yourselfers can, of course, quite easily con-

Breeding Gouldian Finches

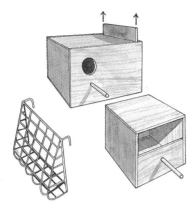

Nest boxes and (lower left) a wire hanger for nesting material.

struct their own nest boxes from ½ inch (1 cm) thick planking. If you have a sliding roof on the nest box it not only will make it easier to inspect the nest, it also will become a much simpler task to clean and disinfect the boxes at the end of the breeding season.

Nest materials can include coconut fibers about 6 to 8 inches (15–20 cm) long, agave fibers, fine hay, and fresh grass. Always ensure that there are adequate nest materials, so that the birds (that are not always particularly brilliant architects) can construct a fitting nursery.

In the wild, Gouldians love bathing when the weather is warm and sunny; in captivity, facilities for bathing also should be available. So that the flying space is kept to a maximum and the water is kept as clean as possible, it is best to use a bird-bath of the type that can be clipped over a door in the cage front. These usually transparent plastic box-like baths are available from pet stores, in several makes. To prevent the cage walls being soiled by splashing water, a little ''porch'' can be made for the birdbath. Also, the container for the dry seed food should be fixed so that it can be replenished from outside the cage. Thus it will be possible to carry out routine cleaning operations with minimum disturbance to the birds.

Depending on the size of the cage, a number of sliding trays (at least two) can be installed in the cage floor. One can be filled with a layer of sand (replacing mini corn cob, see page 32), the other with good garden soil or potting mixture. Such a floor covering, which is probably new to American fanciers, is much used by European bird keepers. The earth filled tray is sprinkled with grass seed in the winter and chickweed seed in the summer. The seed can be watered moderately every other day with a horticultural mist sprayer, and it soon will germinate. As Gouldians quickly panic by each disturbance, the watering is best done through the bath or food container cavity in the cage front.

Bizarre twigs, decorative bark attached to the cage walls, and so on, are not recommended as such commodities are difficult to keep clean. Also, we must not forget that the droppings from Gouldians suffering from enteric infections are very thin and splash like water; a thorough cleaning and disinfection is then only possible if the perches and walls are free from obstructions.

In order to breed and build up one's own ''line'' of birds, the use of breeding cages is most economic; also, the inexperienced fancier can regularly and easily check his birds' health. In a cage, one can be sure that the pair gets its share of green and rearing food, and that the pair is not disturbed by other birds. A cage also will help the birds get to know their owners.

Courtship Behavior in Captivity

If you keep several Gouldians of both sexes together in a garden aviary, it is a good idea to let them choose their own mates. Of course, this only is possible — assuming you want to breed homozygote birds — if all birds in the group are of the same color or mutation.

The first sign that a pair of birds are interested in each other is that they will sit near each other on a perch or horizontal twig and flick their tails. If the hen flies off after a time and the cock follows her, this is another sign that he is seriously interested. Sitting near her on the perch or twig, he will continually serenade her with his song, while "looking her deeply into the eyes"; if interested, the hen also will turn her head towards her "suitor." During his singing concert, the cock bird sits almost bolt upright, with slightly fluffed forehead feathers, and fully erected occiput feathers, making the red, black, or "yellow" mask appear larger and thus hoping to impress his chosen one. Also the breast and belly feathers are somewhat fluffed out, whereas the tail is raised up to expose the blue colored rump, and the head is moved quickly from side to side.

The hen will correspond to this first phase of the courtship by bending her tail and upper body towards the cock. Sometimes the tail can be directed quickly several times towards the male. Should the hen not yet be interested in the proceedings, she will fly quickly away from him, without the behavior described above. Once paired with another cock, the hen may well drive the suitor away aggressively, but usually she just ignores his advances and flies away.

When both birds really are interested in each other, the second phase of the courtship will begin. Again, both birds sit together on a perch, face to face. It is interesting to note that this *particular place* will, from now on, be used for all of the "love games" (phases one and two usually take place several times before the actual pairing at the nest). The upright sitting cock will now utter his "trüit" (ü like the German umlaut ü) call, this being answered by the hen's "weet weet" (ee as in sweet). At the same time, the cock bends his tail at an angle of about 45 degrees towards his "future bride." Again and again as the hen answers his call, he will move his head in the direction of the perch and move it slowly from side to side. And each time he sits upright the hen "answers" with a light, almost charming bow. After these maneuvers have been performed several times, the male begins to sing in earnest, and also to dance. With his back bent he makes whip-

ping motions with his body and nodding motions with his head, but stays in the same place on the perch. Sometimes he may make little jumps in which his feet are detached completely from the perch. After a little time the dance suddenly stops, and the birds sit peacefully next to each other on the perch or twig. Sometimes they will fly several laps of the cage or aviary before returning to the same spot and repeating the dance routine.

After this ceremony, the partners will return to the nest to pair; a kind of behavior that they have in common with, among others, the parrot finches *(Erythrura)*. The hen's readiness to pair first is indicated when she begins to quiver her tail. This behavior also has been seen in the wild. In the cage or aviary it can happen that the cock, on seeing this "come-on" sign from the hen, will fly with a little nest material in his beak onto the roof of the nest box, first peer a few times inside, then enter. Sometimes he becomes so enthusiastic with

One of the signs that a male is in breeding condition is the act of *twirling*. The head is raised high and then jerked towards the tail.

his "house building" that the hen is not allowed in for several hours or even a couple of days!

If the courtship takes place in a larger cage or an aviary containing several pairs, then it can happen that other feathered friends will want to take a look in the nest; both partners that have claimed the nest box as their future nursery will defend it vigorously and chase away any "nosy neighbors." Sometimes, an intruder is attacked so forcibly as to be knocked from the perch to the ground and the defender often will have one of the intruders' feathers in its beak! Fortunately such encounters usually occur only once—the intruder will have learned its lesson. However, in extreme cases where a bird or birds remain aggressive and do not "keep the peace," they should be placed with their partner in a cage exclusively their own.

Once all intruders have been "sorted out," the cock seriously can apply himself to nest building. Personally, I always like to place a handful of nest material in each box, to give the birds "a start" as it were. I make a little hollow in the bundle of nest material with my fist. I do this as some cock birds are quite awful architects; I frequently have seen broods being raised in much too little nest material or even with none at all! In such cases, the eggs can roll all over the place and chances of success are minimized. Luckily, most cock birds make a pretty compact, somewhat globe-shaped little nest in the nest box, which, by the way, is best placed (suspended with little hooks and eyes) against the back wall of the breeding cage in one of the corners with about 4 inches (10 cm) between the top of the box and the ceiling of the cage. The box entrance preferably should face the opposite end of the cage and not towards the wire front. Often the cocks will carry so much nest material that they can hardly enter the nest box! The hen also will assist in the construction of the nest, but the cock will supply all the materials. Once the nest is complete, the remaining nest material must be removed so that an over-enthusiastic cock does not carry so much material to the nest that the eggs are covered and subsequently lost.

Compatible and Incompatible Partners

As we have seen, birds usually will let each other know if they are interested in each other. This is the same for birds in aviary groups as it is for a single pair in a cage. Because we fanciers often want to breed particular color mutations or because we want to breed particularly fine show specimens, we must carry out selective breeding. This means that *we* must choose the partners and only can hope that they will be interested in each other and will breed successfully.

It is essential to place the cock bird in the breeding cage first, and the hen a day later. If the above described courtship behavior takes place, then all is in order. Often, just a few minutes after introducing the hen, the cock will begin to make enthusiastic wiping motions with his beak near the perch; probably the start of phase one of the courtship behavior. If the hen "answers" with her fast tail twisting, we can be assured that all is well. It is also a good sign when the birds sit closely (but not touching) together on a perch or when the hen follows the cock closely.

Unfortunately, it can happen that both birds do not "fancy" each other at all. This will show itself in aggression; beak fencing, chasing aggressively around the aviary, perching as far away from each other as possible, and so on. In such a case, there are two things one can do: give the birds different partners or place each of the pair in a separate cage but where they can see and hear each other. After a week, try reintroducing them, but if it does not work this time we have no option but to try them with different partners.

Egg Laying

The first egg usually is laid about five days after the copulation in the nest. The egg normally is laid in the morning and the hen ordinarily spends a few hours in the nest. After the first egg, a further egg usually is laid each morning until the clutch is complete. Brooding begins in earnest after the third egg.

The clutch averages six eggs, but young hens with their first clutch produce four to five eggs, whereas those that are two or three years old and that already have had several broods, will lay seven to eight eggs. The period between each egg being laid is about 24 hours.

As soon as the clutch is complete, both partners will brood. At night, the hen will brood alone, but during the day the pair will relieve each other. Sometimes it happens that both birds sit together and brood; it is suspected that in such cases, the hen does most of the brooding while the cock keeps her company.

The birds — especially the more inexperienced ones — are somewhat shy and nervous during the brooding process, but will allow nest inspections without too great a risk. Nevertheless, it is advisable to keep nest inspections to a minimum, especially with birds breeding for the first time. The best time to inspect the nest is in the morning, after the hen has been brooding all night and leaves the nest to feed, drink, and stretch her wings.

As already mentioned, the pair will relieve each other in the nest regularly during the day. The bird that is outside first will emit the "nest call," usually while sitting on the roof of the nest box or on the perch close to the entrance; the brooding bird will let out a soft answer and the exchange will take place, often in a period of only a few seconds. The bird being relieved quickly will leave the nest in order to feed and to relax. Still, sometimes both birds will stay in the nest together for awhile. Sometimes the brooding bird is reluctant to leave the eggs and stubbornly will refuse to go outside. In such cases, the bird trying to relieve the other becomes extremely irritated and comes out again. But in general, birds relieve each other satisfactorily each one to two hours during the day.

I know of some cases whereby one of the partners (usually the hen) is so broody that she will not be relieved and will stay on the nest for almost the whole brooding period. However, such situations are infrequent.

As already discussed, the hen broods alone at night; the cock may keep her company in the nest but more usually spends the night close by (on the roof of the nest box or on the entrance perch, for example). I remember a single case in which the cock spent the night in the nest and the hen outside (an inexperienced pair) but, again, this was an exception to the general rule.

After about two weeks the birds will meet frequently in the nest box. This is the time when hatching is expected; usually 16 to 18 days after the beginning of the breeding process. This time may be influenced by the amount of disturbance the birds receive during brooding.

When eggs have been incubated for four to five days, it is possible to tell if they are fertile. Hold them up to the light and, if fertile, you will see the red blood vessels and the dark shadow of the embryo. As the eggs are further incubated, they become less "transparent" as the embryo fills the egg cavity. As long as the embryo is alive, the eggshell will have a white, porcelain-like appearance. If the embryo should die prematurely, the shell will be light-yellow and somewhat transparent. If the embryo dies at a later stage, when it is quite large, the egg will show grayish or brownish blotches and stripes, especially around the air sac. If such an egg is opened it will be seen to contain an evil smelling fluid surrounding the dead embryo. In some cases, especially in the early stages, an egg can dry out and the dead embryo and yolk will stick to the inside of the shell. Such eggs are extremely light, and always roll to the same side up.

Infertile eggs often break very easily and can make a mess of the nest. They should be removed as soon as they are discovered and replaced with artificial eggs.

Do not allow yourself to be discouraged by all the negative points we have mentioned. As long as we provide the right food and conditions for our birds, infertile eggs will be very infrequent. Don't panic if, after a nest inspection, the birds do not return for an hour or so. If the embryos are healthy they will withstand this well. It can happen that both parents will decide to spend the night outside the nest box. As long as this does not happen too frequently, and providing we have optimum temperature in the bird room, the embryos will be able to tolerate this. Experiments have shown that with a night temperature of 64°F (18°C) or below, embryos and newly-hatched young will not survive. However, embryos are not damaged at temperatures between 79 and 82°F (26–28°C) for one or two nights.

It may sometimes happen that a hen will incubate the eggs tightly during the day and evening, but, for reasons unknown to us, will abandon the eggs for the night. In such cases it makes it even more important for us to have the correct temperature in the bird room (see page 14).

Hatching

In most cases the naked, pink-colored young hatch from the egg in the morning hours. Small pieces of eggshell are eaten up by the parents; larger pieces are removed from the nest box and deposited at random on the floor of the cage or aviary.

About one hour after hatching, the youngsters will begin to beg for food. If only one youngster has hatched, the parents usually will ignore its begging call. They first will become really active in providing for the young after two or three days when all the young have hatched. During this time, the hatchlings will survive very well on the egg yolk, which can be seen as a yellow mass in their little bellies. In normal circumstances, two or three young hatch each day — sometimes within 30 minutes of each other — sometimes all five to six in one day!

Most fanciers will have noticed that the parents begin actively to feed the young when these outnumber the still unhatched eggs in the nest.

Thanks to the papillae (see page 58), the parents can see exactly where the food is to be deposited, in spite of the darkness inside the nest box. After about seven to eight days, the nestlings' eyes will begin to open; this process is completed in one or two days. At this time, the young can sit fully upright to beg for food and often sit in a row with their gapes pointing towards the nest entrance. A brood of four, for example, will sit next to each other in a straight row, whereas five or more usually sit in two rows, one behind the other. They can (optically) recognize their parents at this time, a fact you can prove with a little experiment: Before the chicks' eyes are open, tap softly on the nest box, then introduce a finger to the entrance hole. The young will beg as though your finger is a food-bearing parent. However, if the birds are more than 12 days old and you do the same thing, they will not beg and will withdraw in fear deeply into the nest.

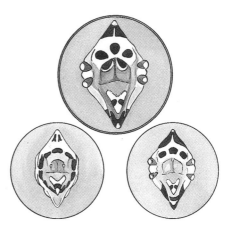

Due to the mouth, tongue and beak markings, and the pear-shaped luminious (bluish) nodules, the parent birds can easily see where to place the food. Note the striking similarity of the mouth markings of the Gouldian finch (top) and the red-headed parrot finch (right). Other Australian grassfinches, such as the masked grassfinch (left), don't have the nodules on the outside angle of the beak, while the markings inside the mouth are clearly different.

Breeding Gouldian Finches

The following is a summary of the gradual stages in development in the nestlings:
• At four to five days old: the skin color darkens from reddish pink to grayish-blue.
• At seven days old: the beginnings of the tail and wing feathers are visible.
• At nine days old: the back and flank feathers are visible.
• At 12–14 days old: the tail and wing feathers break out of the feather follicles; breast and belly follicles and head follicles are visible.
• 14–16 days old: the wing feathers are almost completely out of the follicles.
• At 18–19 days old: the whole ot the upper side is feathered. In contrast, the underside still has unfeathered parts, which will be fully feathered in a further two to three days.
• At 22–23 days old: fully feathered, the young leave the nest. At this time the fledgelings open their wings and are full of spirit; it sounds like they are throwing a party in the nest box!

Once fledged, the young have a difficult time for a couple of days and may find it hard to get up on a perch. But after three to four days practice, they will be flying round their cage or aviary as though they had been doing it for years.

Turning to a less tasteful topic; unlike many bird species, Gouldian parents do *not* remove the youngsters' droppings from the nest. The youngsters deposit their droppings at the edge of the nest. At four to five days of age, each time they defecate, they will "reverse" to the side of the nest and "smear" it with droppings. The result of this behavior — in which the body is pressed against the side of the nest — is that the nest walls grow steadily higher.

It is easy to check if the droppings dry out well. If they remain wet and smeary, there is a chance that one or more of the young is suffering from diarrhea, probably caused by incorrect feeding. Of course, the diet should be improved immediately. Extra vitamin B12 or a good vitamin supplement containing vitamin B12 is recommended highly.

When fresh nest material is offered, the parents frequently will reline the nest like new. This will, of course, do no harm. Even though the young may have diarrhea (which also can be seen by the condition of their bodies; an inflamed, red liver, which can be seen through the skin, and a temporary postponement of growth), the parents will continue to feed them. Ensure, therefore, that the rearing food is correct and supply vitamins if necessary.

Now for a few remarks about so-called "I-want-it-all" birds. One or two such young Gouldians sometimes occur in a nest and at 16–18 days ot age they will push themselves forward so that they sit right next to or under the entrance hole. Each time the parents come with food, they begin to loudly beg for tidbits. The noteworthy thing here is that the parents will ignore them and not offer them any food. These "I-want-it-all" birds soon lose weight and, driven by hunger, will leave the nest in a couple of days. We can try to put them back in the nest, but this usually does not help much and after a few seconds they are out again. To avoid undue disturbance to the young still in the nest, it is best to attempt to hand-feed such problem youngsters. Once they reach "normal strength," and are again as fit as the young still in the nest, they can be reintroduced. As rearing food I use Avi-Start (L/M Animal Farms), which is excellent. Usually the "early fliers" will then stay with their brothers and sisters, but if they go outside again we will have to further feed them by hand, until the rest of the brood is flying around in the cage or aviary.

Rearing

When everything runs normally in the nest, the young will fledge, fully feathered in 22–23 days, witĥ the exception of any "I-want-it-all" birds that frequently show feathers still in the follicles. These latter birds should be given a vitamin supplement containing biotin (vitamin H) to help them develop. We should keep a close eye on

Breeding Gouldian Finches

them, as these "eccentrics" have the habit of hiding in corners of the cage or aviary, under or against seed hoppers, on the edge of a drinking dish or a bath or similar, as they can hardly fly. It is interesting to note that such youngsters frequently sit in the water and take a bath. As they are poorly feathered this can lead quickly to death. In order to avoid this risk, I remove the bath during the first couple of days. Prevention is better than cure — I also have seen fully feathered young eagerly take a bath, but this really is not advisable during the first few days after leaving the nest. The parent birds often do not notice the "I-want-it-all" youngsters in their little corners and they thus get neglected, they starve, quickly weaken, and may soon die from hunger and/or cold. We thus have to help these little bunglers. Unfortunately it is not easy to care for them in an outside aviary. However, in a breeding cage, install a few low perches. Newly-fledged youngsters, including the "I-want-it-all" birds, will sit on these perches and the parents will find them easily.

If using an outdoor aviary, it is wise to ensure that the young spend the nights in the night shelter, at least for the first four to five days. In rainy or excessively cold weather, it is best not to allow the birds access to the outdoor flight.

After fledging, the young usually never return

A fledgling begging for food.

to the nest box — even to spend the night. I know of a few cases where the parent birds lead the young to the nest box in the evenings, and they spend the night there.

After about three weeks, we can regard the young Gouldians as independent; it frequently happens that two or four days out of the nest the young will start feeding themselves (soaked millet spray suspended close to the floor, good rearing food in shallow dishes, and so on) — but we must not take this "independence" too literally! At first the young will "play" with the food quite a lot; the "first efforts" at feeding. It goes without saying then, that the young are totally dependent on the parent birds for food for the first 14 days at least. As long as the parent birds do not begin a new brood, it is best to leave the young with them as long as possible, that is to say, at least three weeks. If the parents begin a new brood during this three weeks, but do not show too much agression towards their older brood, then we still can leave them all together. It is recommended that young birds are introduced, as early as possible, to the breeding behavior, nest building, and feeding of their brothers and sisters. Good example begets good results!

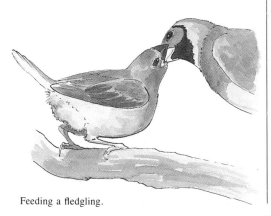

Feeding a fledgling.

Breeding Gouldian Finches

We can do it another way: when the young are three to four days out of the nest, remove the nest box so that the parents (temporarily) are unable to start a new brood. As soon as the young are independent, then they are removed to a separate, roomy flight (minimum 30 by 20 by 20 inches (76 × 51 × 51 cm). You must decide from experience which of these two methods is best for you.

At 45–50 days of age, the young should be transferred to a larger flight, 10 by 7 by 7 feet (3 x 2 x 2 m), so that they have opportunity to fully develop their bodies through adequate exercise. If you have more than 45–50 youngsters, you must use more flights to avoid excessive squabbling (over the perches, food hoppers, and so on) and the related stress that can develop. For this reason, I do what many canary breeders do; I provide numerous short perches of 10 inches (25 cm) long in a row along each of the two longer sides of the flight. Two birds can then sit side by side, undisturbed. Another method is to divide longer perches up into "apartments" — again about 10 inches (25 cm) wide with squares of cardboard or similar. Two birds can then settle in each compartment without disturbance from their neighbors.

Soon the young will be experiencing their first molt. Remember that in addition to the usual good seed mixture, the birds should have access to a good brand of soft food, soaked millet spray, sprouted seeds, fresh greens (free from insecticides), and cuttle bone.

Bird Banding

If you want to build a pedigree line of birds and study methods of heredity, then it is essential that you keep meticulous records. Record cards can be attached to each cage with a thumbtack. On the card we record the details of the parents (numbers or letters on the band) as well as notes on their breeding and rearing performances in the past and present. Notes on the young are also included — their behavior, good and bad characteristics, and whatever else is thought important.

Young Gouldians can be legbanded with closed rings (made from colored plastic or aluminum) on the seventh to ninth day after hatching.

Putting leg bands on Gouldians is not difficult. There are four toes to each foot, three pointing forward, the fourth pointing to the rear. To start, wash your hands in warm water. Hold the bird in your left palm if you are right-handed (left-handed persons do the reverse). Squeeze the three front toes carefully together between the thumb and forefinger (wetting them with water or saliva will make this easier) so that they lay in line with the "ball of the foot." Take the band between the thumb and forefinger of the right hand and push it gently over the toes and the ball of the foot. The

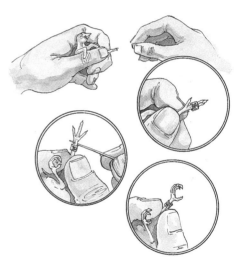

Banding a chick (clockwise from the top). Take the bird's foot between your fingers with the back toe pointing toward the back and the other toes held together and pointing toward the front. Rub a *little* petroleum jelly or salad oil on the toe. Now place the band over the three front toes, slide it backwards, over the back toe, and continue a little further up the leg as well. If the back toe is still caught under the band, release it with a somewhat pointed matchstick. The band is now correctly positioned around the chick's leg. After you clean the leg, put the chick back into the nest.

hindmost toe is now caught between the band and the leg. Take a somewhat sharpened matchstick and put it gently under the toe to liberate it. It is best to visit an experienced breeder and watch the way he or she does it. If you have an agile and steady hand, the job is easy.

Colony Breeding

I personally consider an indoor or outdoor aviary, populated with a varied and colorful collection of compatible bird species, one of the most challenging and interesting facets of the hobby. Keeping Gouldians in an aviary is not easy; it is always difficult to maintain adequate control and breeding results are almost never as good as those carried out in the controlled environment of a breeding cage.

However, if you wish to enjoy the attractive colors and the fascinating behavior of Gouldians, without laying too much value on producing large numbers of young, then an aviary is the ideal choice. If you require reasonably good results in an aviary, then this can be achieved by concentrating on one color mutation (i.e., keep all red-headed or all black-headed together). We thus have homozygote (see page 68) pairs that will produce young similar in appearance to the parents.

Colony breeding therefore means that we keep several pairs of Gouldians together in an aviary and allow them to breed. As fanciers, we thus interfere very little with the *normal procedure,* which is left totally "in the hands" of the birds themselves. The birds will select their own partners and seek out a nest box that is acceptable to them — these are aspects that, viewed from a distance, give the fancier a great deal of pleasure. Those fanciers who live in our warmer states and who have, especially, the opportunity to keep their birds in outdoor aviaries for the whole year round soon will notice how captivating and lively Gouldians are. In our "colder" states, well-acclimatized birds can be kept in outdoor aviaries from May through September. In the Netherlands,

Germany, England, Denmark, and other European countries, Gouldians also are kept successfully and bred in outdoor aviaries — as long as they have well-constructed, rain and windproof night shelter attached.

Even so, I will not recommend this method; in colder areas, the birds should be brought into heated indoor accommodations in the fall and winter, and protected from drafts, to which Gouldians are particularly sensitive.

Experience has shown that four pairs of Gouldians are best kept in an aviary with an outdoor flight 13 feet long, 4 feet wide and 6 feet high ($4 \times 1.2 \times 1.8$ m) and a night shelter 4 by 4 by 6 feet ($1.2 \times 1.2 \times 1.8$ m); larger aviaries can, of course, contain more pairs. Give at least the same number of nest boxes (all the same type) as there are pairs of birds, and do not place them too close to each other; there must be enough flying room left for the birds. Install the nest boxes and give adequate nesting material towards the latter part of spring, when the daylight hours are lengthening and chances of frost are past. Give a great deal of thought to the diet and provide (as always) a good seed mixture, a good brand of soft egg food/rearing food, and soaked millet spray.

Some Practical Tips

• If you are taking the breeding of Gouldian finches seriously, you not only will require adequate breeding cages and utensils, but also a few pairs of society finches *and* extra cock Gouldians. It sometimes happens that an introduced pair will refuse or fail to mate, let alone produce a clutch of eggs, even after a month or so together! Try introducing another cock bird to the pair. Although the hen rarely will pair with this new suitor, his presence will be enough to produce a positive reaction! The same is true for the original partner cock, who sees the newly-introduced cock as a direct rival. Shortly after the introduction of a new cock, the couple most likely will become aggressive towards him and make his life difficult. The

Breeding Gouldian Finches

"intruder" should then be removed immediately from the cage. The stimulatory effect of this intrusion on the original pair means that in most cases normal courtship and mating will follow; sometimes I have seen the first egg in a well-constructed nest just ten days later. The pair must, of course, be left in peace and quiet so that a good relationship can develop — in particular, do not look in the nest box too frequently!

• Sometimes, checking the eggs will reveal that they are all infertile. Such eggs (which will make a mess in the nest if they break) must be removed. If all eggs are removed the hen usually will begin with a new clutch within a few days. In case just one or two eggs are left, share these out with another breeding pair or foster them to a pair of society finches.

So that we know which is which among the youngsters, we should foster out red-headed Gouldians to black-headed parents and so on. Gouldians rarely, for some reason or other, will rear successfully a single chick in the nest. In such cases it is best to foster it out.

• It may happen occasionally that the adult cock will throw the young out of the nest as soon as they hatch. Experiments have shown that usually stress, or overrich food, resulting in hyperactivity is the cause. It also is possible that the cock is not in the same phase of the breeding cycle as the hen; maybe he will want to start again with courtship, nest building, and mating. The fancier obviously must control the diet and keep a close watch on the birds at all times, studying them especially in the early part of the breeding season; both partners must reach the various phases of the breeding cycle together.

• Dead-in-shell-victims can be avoided by keeping the correct humidity at all times, by providing the parents — that should not be too young and should be from a healthy strain — with an adequate varied diet, rich in vitamins and minerals, and by keeping their accommodations clean and as sterile as possible (to avoid *Salmonella*).

• Young birds in the nest suffering from diarrhea soon will make the nest wet and dirty. Remove the young from the nest and change the soiled nest material for fresh material, providing some extra under the nest box for the parents to use; replace the young. Dissolve the appropriate antibiotics in the drinking water (see page 50). Frequent nest inspections will help you intercept such infections before they go too far.

• Should the rearing food be inadequate, or if the parent birds are negligent in their feeding duties, one can usually see this, especially in the first few days. The crop will appear empty or almost empty but sometimes filled with seed instead of rearing food, and sometimes dull, wrinkled skin is evident. Ensure that adequate soft food and soaked millet are available, as youngsters only a few days old are unable to fully digest seeds. If the young are suffering from diarrhea (see above), this usually can be seen by their dirty vents. The feeding must, in this case, also be corrected or drastically changed.

• As can occur in grass parakeets, Gouldian finches also can suffer from an air-blown crop. Experience has shown us that we should not try to treat this, but we must take absolute care with the diet (Is it too dry? Is there too much seed?). Once the diet is in order, the air quickly will disperse from the crop, without any further intervention.

In nestling Gouldians, four to five days and older, and other finches, including canaries, one sometimes comes across white, cheese-like patches along the roof of the mouth and throat area (easy to see when they gape for food). This condition is caused by *Trichomonas,* a microscopic protozoan parasite, which, in severe cases, can be fatal. The patient quickly will weaken, lose its appetite, have a shortness of breath, and have thin droppings. I have noticed that this condition occurs more frequently in outdoor aviaries than in cages. Although the life cycle, and the manner of transmission (droppings?) is not yet thoroughly known, the disease occurs in all bird species, especially pigeons (where it is called canker) and birds of prey (where it is called frounce). The veterinarian will prescribe dimetridazole (Emtryl) or metronidazole (Flagyl) as a treatment for the disease.

Society Finches (Bengalese) as Foster Parents

Now and again, we will come across parent Gouldians who, for one reason or another, will not or cannot adequately brood their eggs or rear their hatchlings. In such cases, society finches are essential — there is no excuse for allowing the eggs or young of healthy Gouldians to die.

Society finches or Bengalese, as they are called by the English, are domesticated finches belonging to the genus *Lonchura* ("lance bearer," referring to the birds' long-pointed tail feathers) in the family Estrildidae. These finches were "created" centuries ago by the Chinese, probably from crossings with striated finches (*Lonchura striata*) and sharp-tailed finches (*Lonchura acuticauda*). The society finches are well known as outstanding cage and aviary birds, and anyone wishing to start keeping finches can do no better than gaining experience with these lively and interesting birds, before advancing to more ambitious projects.

Over the years, time and again, society finches have proven to be outstanding foster parents to many finch species. Research by, among others, the German ornithologist Professor Dr. Karl Immelmann has shown that fostering can have a detrimental effect with regard to imprinting, especially when the young are left *too long* with the society finches.

Indeed, Immelmann's studies deal largely with zebra finches versus society finches, but one can suppose that the most important results of Immelmann's research — including imprinting — can just as well also apply to Gouldians, although so far nothing concrete has emerged.

Immelmann's experiments showed that male zebra finches reared by society finches, imagined themselves to be society finches when they were adult and their courtship behavior was more like that of a society finch that that of a zebra finch. A similar effect was seen as foster-reared zebra finch hens made amorous advances to male society finches. However, a zebra finch male reared by society finches would eventually mate with a "normal" zebra finch hen after a period of time, if the pair was placed in a special cage without society finches.

Healthy society finches are essential to the Gouldian breeder. The idea that Gouldians reared by foster parents will not be interested in their own species is untrue; thus the opposite to the tests of zebra finches versus society finches. In other words, the imprinting, which one is so anxious about, from the foster parents on the Gouldians seems to have very little or no influence. Of course, if the fostered Gouldians are kept together with the society finches well into their adulthood, then such problems may occur.

Society finches breed most satisfactorily in breeding cages 16 by 13 by 16 inches (41 × 33 × 41 cm). Over the years, many have followed

Society Finches have proven to be outstanding foster parents to many finches, including Gouldians.

Breeding Gouldian Finches

Teague's example: three pairs of society finches, with a strain of ten pairs of Gouldians. The society finches are given facilities to breed at the same time as the Gouldians. Feeding (especially of protein-rich food) and care are the same as that required by the Gouldians, with the exception of charcoal granules, which I never give to society finches. Outside the breeding season, it is recommended that society finches also are housed in roomy flights.

Eggs from Gouldians preferably should be fostered to society finches when both pairs begin brooding at about the same time; although a difference of two to three days (definitely not longer!) should not matter too much. Mixed clutches and chicks are best avoided, although it has been done (with mixed success). After you remove the society finch clutch and replace it with that of the Gouldians, it can happen that the hen society finch will lay another one or two eggs; these should be removed and given to other society finches to brood. The Gouldian eggs should be gently marked with a little cross, using a felt-tipped pen,

so that you do not get the eggs mixed up. In general, society finches will accept foster eggs or young at any time during their breeding cycle, but the best results are achieved when the two pairs are synchronized. Disasters are likely to occur if, for example, you place three-day-old young next to young that are eight to ten days old!

The breeding process runs similarly to that performed by the Gouldians. After about five weeks, young society finches should be separated from their parents and placed in roomy flight cages.

As aviculturists, we must not misuse the situation; in other words we must not produce clutch after clutch of Gouldians, to be fostered to society finches. Our breeding efforts must strive for quality rather than quantity!

Many fanciers have noticed that some foster parents, like some Gouldians, for one reason or another fail to feed the young properly or even throw them out of the nest. Experience has shown that these abandoned young will, once reared to adulthood, show similar behavior. This phenomenon most likely is due to a genetic deficiency.

Left, a yellow- or orange-headed Gouldian; right, a ▶ white-breasted mutation. Other varieties in addition to the white-breasted are blue-, cobalt-, and lilac-breasted.

If Your Gouldian Finch Gets Sick

Hospital Cages

One of the most important pieces of emergency equipment to have in case a bird gets sick is the hospital cage. Although hospital cages can be purchased on the market, it is more economical and not difficult to make one yourself. A simple box, 28 inches high by 16 inches wide by 20 inches deep (70 × 40 × 51 cm) is constructed from good quality plywood. Install three 60 watt light bulbs each working independently of the other. This will allow maintenance of the correct temperatures — a constant 85 to 90°F (29–32°C) whatever the season.

An easy-to-read thermometer should be attached to one wall (as far away from the light bulbs as possible so that you get a true reading of the air temperature). It is best to have a sliding tray in the floor of the cage; this can be covered with a good layer of sand, which should be replaced twice a day as the feces of a sick bird are likely to be infected with disease organisms (dispose of by burying or burning first to destroy organisms). A wire screen installed just above the floor will allow the bird's droppings to fall through and will help prevent the bird from reinfecting itself (the wire screen should be removed and disinfected daily). Food and water can be supplied through a small door at one end of the cage. Water especially is important to sick birds kept in the relatively high temperature of the hospital cage and the bird hopefully will drink a lot, which will contribute towards its cure. The areas beneath and adjacent to the light bulbs should be covered preferably with a nonflammable material to prevent any chance of fire.

Although the bird is being kept warm in the hospital cage, it is very important that we have an

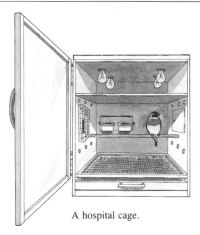

A hospital cage.

efficient air exchange. Ventilate by having a few air holes at each end of the cage. Although not entirely essential, it will make things much easier to clean the cage if the roof or front is hinged, or removable so that you have easy access to all corners of the cage. After your sick bird recovers, the cage must be scrubbed thoroughly and disinfected, inside and out (on no account forget to disconnect the electricity supply before doing this!). If possible, dry it out in natural sunlight, before putting it away or using it for another patient.

The Air Sac Mite

The air sac mite *(Sternostoma tracheacolum),* is a blood-sucking arthropod that frequently affects Gouldians and, to a lesser extent, canaries and other finch species. In the fairly recent past, this parasite was the cause of many Gouldian deaths, and included adult as well as young birds. The mites infest the trachea, lungs, and air sacs.

An infestation can occur in a mild or acute form. The mild form shows no specific symptoms other than the usual (for many infections) puffing out of feathers, ceasing to sing, moping, and slowly losing body condition.

◀ Above: left and center, two black-headed "normal" or wild colored males; right, a red-headed, white-breasted normal green-bodied male. Below: left, a red-headed yellow-bodied white-breasted male; center, a red-headed dilute-bodied male; right, a yellow-headed yellow-bodied white-breasted male.

If Your Gouldian Finch Gets Sick

At a later stage, as the mites infect the lungs and air sacs, the bird will develop obvious breathing difficulties (dyspnea). The bird will make swallowing noises, will wipe its beak repeatedly on perches or twigs, and will attempt to remove the mites from its air passages by coughing and spluttering. As the infection develops, the bird's labored breathing will be accompanied by wheezing and peeping sounds, intermingled with little sneezes. In acute cases, the bird can suffocate from a literal plug of mites in the air passages. A microscopic examination will reveal numerous, dark-colored mites in the nostrils, the trachea, and all respiratory organs. Young mites usually are found in the nostrils.

For a long time it was thought that the birds expired through loss of blood, but this is not true; death occurs as a result of exhaustion caused by extreme dyspnea due to the presence of numerous mites in the trachea. The presence of the mites in a live bird is difficult to ascertain. Since a tracheal swab is required, this job is best left to a veterinarian.

In *Bird World*, July 1987, Roger W. Harlin, DVM points out: "if you wet down the bird and shine a strong light through the neck, you can see tiny dark dots along the trachea."

Young mites can be expelled from the beak and nostrils through coughing and sneezing and easily can affect other birds, through the food, water, or even by direct inhalation. Mites or their eggs are never, at least very seldom, found in the birds' droppings, so there is no diagnosis to be found from that angle. We must be able to differentiate between a mite infestation and other respiratory conditions, such as diptheria (usually in canaries, other finch species, and doves, but rarely in Gouldians), trachea-worms, aspergillosis, and colds.

Treatment: In Gouldian finches, the treatment of an air sac mite infestation is fairly problematical. One method is to use an insecticidal strip (of the type used for killing houseflies). A new strip should be suspended outside for a cou-

ple of hours (to dissipate the initial release of toxic fumes that could be highly dangerous to the birds). A whole strip should be used in a room with a floor area of not less than 300 square feet (90 sq. m). In smaller rooms, the strip should be cut into appropriately smaller portions. Birds should not be able to have direct contact with the strip, which is hung in the room containing the cages. The strip should be suspended in the room for four to six hours per day over a period of five days, after which the birds should be cured.

There are a few more methods that can be tried. One of these is what I call the "shake and bake" method; this has saved many of my birds from an almost certain death. The patient is placed in a paper bag containing a sprinkling of one teaspoonful of five percent carbaryl (Sevin) powder. Not being very happy in the bag, the bird will flutter its wings and produce an effective dusting. An exposure of just five to ten seconds is adequate. Release the bird immediately back into its cage, which should be placed in a well-ventilated area. Do not be anxious about the powder getting in the birds' eyes. As you probably know, birds possess the so named "third eyelid" (nictitating membrane), which protects the eye from irritation and abrasion. A complete cure usually is accomplished after a few days.

M. Partington, DVM states in *The Canary and Finch Journal* (Second Quarter, 1988): "Ivermectine (Eqvalan) affords a one-time method of treatment. The diluted (2.0 mg/ml) Eqvalan is injected at a dosage of 0.01 cc per 30 grams of body weight. Ivermectine is not yet approved by the FDA for use in birds. This dosage is given only as a guideline of what has been found to be relatively efficaceous in small birds in previous careful administration."

Dr. Harlin warns however: "Ivermectine has been used very successfully. The entire flock must be treated at the same time and the premises cleaned. Have your veterinarian treat the birds or prepare the mixture for you for home treatment. Some forms of Ivermectine dissipate rapidly and

If Your Gouldian Finch Gets Sick

should be used within a specific time period after mixing. Inquire as to usage if you treat them at home. Ivermectine can be easily overdosed and losses can be alarming if it is used carelessly. Be sure that a professional has advised you as to the mixture or has mixed it for you."

Dr. M.D. Murray, an Australian veterinarian, has another method of treatment against air sac mites. In *Australian Veterinary Journal* (1966, Vol. 42, pp. 262–264), he suggests mixing 0.04 gram of carbaryl, with 50 grams of seed mixture. To improve chances of the powder being taken, he further suggests mixing 1 ml. cod-liver oil so that the powder adheres to the seed. This seed is given for 48 hours in the first week, then for a period of 24 hours each in the second and third weeks. In view of the results quoted, this method also is to be recommended.

Aspergillosis

This is an unpleasant disease to which many bird species, including Gouldians, are susceptible. The disease starts when the spores of certain fungi, notably *Aspergillus fumigatus*, are breathed into the air passages. Certain plants, such as those belonging to the genus *Asperula*, can help bring about this fungal infection. Moldy bread and seeds, musty hay, chaff, or straw, and similar items are also a potential source of aspergillosis infection. The spores produce poisonous toxins that damage the mucous membranes in the various parts of the respiratory tract and in the air sacs. Eventually, a yellow, cheese-like pus develops that will prevent adequate respiration. The bird may shake its head and stretch out its neck regularly, as if trying to dislodge a blockage. The bird loses its appetite, becomes morose and weak, and eventually will die.

To date, no wholly satisfactory cure for aspergillosis has been discovered, though a good avian veterinarian often can prescribe relieving treatment. The answer is to ensure that your birds are never put in a position where they can contract the disease. Always use fresh, clean seeds, never old or moldy ones. Do not give spilled seed a chance to get moldy; clean the aviary frequently and regularly, sweeping up all spilled food. Maintain an optimum humidity but not at the expense of good ventilation. Try to prevent dust and plant spores from blowing into the aviary. If possible do not use hay, straw, or chaff near the birds, but if this is absolutely necessary, only use freshly dried, sweet smelling materials, not those that have been stored for long periods in musty conditions. In the event of a case of aspergillosis among your birds, the aviary and its surroundings should be subjected to an intensive inspection to try and discover the source of the infection. Remove the source if found, then thoroughly clean all bird accomodations and disinfect by spraying with a 1 percent solution of copper sulfate before the birds are reintroduced.

Canker or *Trichomonas*

Canker is caused by a microscopic protozoan parasite called *Trichomonas* that affects many species of birds, especially the young. The *Trichomonas* organisms spend their whole lives in the liver, intestines, and, especially, the throat and crop. Frequently the disease causes cheese-like deposits inside the mouth and throat area and sick birds gasp for breath. Gouldian finches, especially the nestlings, can be infected; the symptoms include: gasping for breath, empty crops, and weakness. You should consult an avian veterinarian immediately (see page 42).

Treatment: The treatment of choice is a good antibiotic mixed with dimetridazole (Emtryl) or metronidazole (Flagyl). Be sure to follow your veterinarian's directions carefully. As at least three quarters of the wild populations of pigeons and doves are estimated to be infected with *Trichomonas* it is very important to protect the roofs of garden aviaries as much as possible to prevent doves and other wild birds gaining access. Do not offer ordinary drink or bathwater at the same time as medicated water (see page 51).

If Your Gouldian Finch Gets Sick

Colds

A cold is not caused directly by the cold weather itself, but excessively low temperatures can cause stress, which reduces the resistance to certain organisms, commonly those associated with respiratory infections. As well as exposure to low temperatures, "colds" can be brought about by drafts, vitamin A deficiency, other forms of stress, coupled with an invasion of pathogenic viruses, bacteria, or fungi. A bird with a respiratory infection will have typical symptoms: rapid, audible respiration (wheezing, clicking); its beak will be open and its panting will cause its tail to go up and down. The bird will sneeze and cough, have a nasal discharge, and lose its appetite. In most cases is will also puff out its feathers and sit moping in some corner.

A bird suffering from a respiratory disease requires immediate treatment if pneumonia is to be avoided (pneumonia is a natural progression from many respiratory infections if they are untreated and/or if the cause(s) of stress are not removed; pneumonia is an infection deep in the lungs that is very difficult to cure). Remove the sick bird from the cage or aviary and place it in a warm environment (hospital cage). Remove any discharge or encrustations from around the nostrils by gently dabbing with a cotton ball. Use a fine mist sprayer to spray a warm mist of water into the cage to soothe and moisturize the inflamed mucous membranes (a standard vaporizer available from your drugstore is ideal). In any case, you should consult an avian veterinarian who may prescribe additional treatment. As always, check that accommodations, location, food, and temperature are up to standard.

Diarrhea

A bird suffering from diarrhea has not necessarily contracted an infectious disease but may just have an intestinal disorder. However, the bird should be placed immediately in a hospital cage maintained at 90°F (32°C), with a wire mesh separating the bird from the floor. Strict hygiene of the cage interior and utensils is very important.

Various factors can cause intestinal upsets in Gouldians; for example, bad food, obesity, respiratory infection, excessive heat, chill, viral or bacterial outbreaks in the intestines (for example: *E. coli, Pasteurella, Salmonella),* or an excess of protein in the diet.

Visible symptoms of impaired intestinal function include listlessness, "hunching," and diarrhea (the vent is wet and the feathers in this area will adhere to each other). In serious cases, the bird no longer will rest on a perch but will take to the floor, often sitting in a corner with its head tucked under its wing. The droppings will be very watery and can, depending on the type of infection, be whitish, green, yellow, or fawn in color. An avian veterinarian should be consulted immediately.

Treatment: The veterinarian can prescribe various antibiotics. Evans and Fidler (see Literature and Addresses, page 77) advise "0.4 g *aureo-*

Oral medication can be administered by using a small *plastic* medicine or eye dropper.

If Your Gouldian Finch Gets Sick

mycin, or *spectinomycin,* or *terramycin,* together with 1.5 ml of a 33 percent solution of sulphamezathine in 56 ml (2 fluid ounces) of water.'' This treatment should be carried out over five days and should replace the drinking water.

E. coli Infections

Gouldian finches can have problems with *Escherichia coli,* gram-negative bacteria (generally abbreviated *E. coli*). The principal victims of *E. coli,* are humans, but birds are not immune. *E. coli,* in spite of common belief among many bird keepers, are *not* normal residents of a bird's intestines and, if they spread to the lungs, liver, and heart, fatalities will occur.

As always, prevention is infinitely better than cure and good hygiene should be the order of the day, *every* day. Wash your hands before you move birds, prepare food, inspect nests, or carry out any other activities with your birds. Prevent fecal contamination by keeping all cage and aviary furnishings and utensils spotless (clean and disinfect frequently and regularly — this cannot be repeated often enough!).

Treatment: Offer one to two drops of Kaopectate or Pepto-Bismol every four hours, administered with a plastic medicine dropper. This will coat the inflamed gut linings and soothe them. If no improvement occurs within six hours, seek immediate veterinary advice (antibiotic treatment may be necessary).

Egg Binding

This problem rarely occurs in birds that are housed and fed in ideal conditions. Egg binding is the term applied to the problem in which a hen bird is unable to lay an egg that is ready to come out. She will look sick, hunched up (usually on the cage floor, seldom in the nest), will barely move, and often can be caught easily in the hand. If you gently palpitate the lower abdomen, you will feel the problem — the stuck egg.

In normal conditions, the egg spends no more than 24 hours in the wide section of the ovary leading to the cloaca, and the cloaca itself. The muscles in the lower part of the ovary push the egg forward at the proper time and then, a short time later, entirely out of the body via the vent. A bird may be suffering from undue stress from colds, chills, drafts, overbreeding, frights, or from poor muscle tone (old age, out of condition), or a deficiency of various dietary constituents. The affected bird will try very hard to lay the egg, but in vain.

Sometimes, a malfunction in the calcium depositing mechanism or, indeed, an actual deficiency of calcium in the hen's diet, will cause the production of shell-less or soft-shelled eggs (often called "wind eggs"). Such eggs often also are a cause of a form of egg binding as the weak or absent shell tends to get stuck because the cloaca muscles cannot get an adequate grip on the soft mass.

Under normal circumstances, egg binding is totally preventable. Again, all of the usual points must be considered before breeding commences. Bring the bird into top condition with a balanced diet containing all of the necessary macronutrients and micronutrients (good seeds, green food, sprouted seed, vitamins and minerals, cuttle bone). As a further precaution against wind eggs, ensure that your birds get enough calcium phosphate. Commercial bird grits contain adequate key minerals, and during breeding a little bread soaked in water with grated cheese may be appreciated.

Never try to breed birds too early in the season (especially those housed outside). Low temperatures are a major cause of egg binding. Immature females should not be bred as they are likely candidates for egg binding (see page 31).

Treatment: Providing you act fast enough, egg binding is, fortunately, entirely curable. For lubrication introduce a few drops of warm mineral oil into the cloaca, using a plastic dropper. Next place the affected bird in a hospital cage or somewhere where you can maintain a temperature of about 90° F (32° C). Alternatively, consult an avian veterinarian who, with the use of certain medicines, may be able to stimulate the bird into laying.

Mites

Feather mites can be divided into two major types; the nondisease mites that live on the skin as well as the feathers and very small mites that burrow into the shaft and the follicle.

The first type, *Syringophilus bipectioratus,* may be found in wild birds and many domestic birds including canaries and other finches, sometimes Gouldians. It feeds on skin and feather debris and can cause irritation that leads to feather plucking. The second type, *Dermoglyphus elongatus,* is slightly more serious as it actually burrows into the feather structure, causing damage.

The best therapy against feather mites is excellent hygiene. Keep the cages as clean as possible and allow the birds adequate bathing facilities. Keep your aviaries as inaccessible as possible to wild birds. Such precautions also will help control the red bird-mite *Dermanyssus gallinae.* This so-called surface-dwelling mite does not live on the body of its victim but hides during the day in cracks and crevices around the cage or aviary, emerging under the protection of darkness to feed on the birds' blood. A single mite does not, of course, take a great deal of blood, but in great numbers these pests can cause untold damage, weakening your birds and spreading disease. Nesting birds and their young can be constantly and severely irritated by the bites of these mites. The mites themselves are capable of surviving for months without a blood meal. At such times they are difficult to detect as they are translucent, only taking on the red color from the blood they feed on. At temperatures of 68° F (20° C) and with a regular blood supply, the mites can reproduce every five days, so, in ideal conditions for them, it does not take long for an aviary or bird room to be

infested with millions of them. They can survive in outdoor aviaries even in times of severe frost. The mites often are introduced by wild birds (it only takes a single, gravid female mite to start off an infestation), or they can be brought in with new stock.

It is important to keep watch for signs of a mite infestation so that it may quickly be dealt with in its initial stages. Examine your cages and aviaries at each cleaning session (a magnifying glass may help you here). Of course, the fewer cracks and crevices there are for the mites to hide in, the better. One way to detect an infestation is to cover a cage at night with a white cloth and look for the mites in the folds of the cloth the next day (they appear as tiny red spots). If mites are present the cloth should be burned.

Treatment: If you discover an infestation of red bird-mite among your stock, you must treat all cages, aviaries, bird rooms, and adjacent areas without delay. Many kinds of insecticides are suitable. If birds are present, it is best to use those based on pyrethrin (a natural substance made from the pyrethrum flower, a kind of chrysanthemum), which is harmless to the birds but is effective against ticks, lice, fleas, and other invertebrate pests as well as mites. In addition to spraying a water-based pyrethrin product on all surfaces of cages and aviaries, nest box equipment, and adjacent areas (paying particular attention to areas in which the mites can hide), your birds can be dusted with a pyrethrin powder, paying special attention to the neck, around the vent, and under the wings. Do not return the birds to their quarters until the insecticide has dried out. A repeat treatment after five days will eliminate any pests that hatch from eggs in the meantime. Such a treatment usually is adequate for many months at least and often permanent, but always remain vigilant in case of a reinfestation.

Molt

Molting, or changing of the feathers, is a natural phenomenon that all birds go through annual-

If Your Gouldian Finch Gets Sick

ly. It is necessary for old feathers, suffering from wear and tear, to be replaced with new ones. The condition of the plumage rests on many factors. Infestations of parasites, effects of weather and wind (temperature, humidity, photoperiod), preening, nesting, the young creeping between them for warmth, and other activities all take their toll.

A normal, problem-free molt is dependent on the season, temperature, and diet. It may be noted that the molt is often more intense after a warm spring and a good beginning to the summer than it is during cold and wet months. In some cases a bird seems very eager to molt, as if it can't wait to get rid of its old tatty feathers and replace them with fine, sleek, new ones. It will fluff out continually and shake its old feathers, sometimes even plucking the odd annoying one out with its beak and clearly deriving some pleasure from doing so! In most cases however, the molt is a restful time for a bird, especially one that has just passed through a very hectic breeding season. Research has shown that, during the molt, a bird's body temperature is somewhat higher than normal, but if the molt is unsatisfactory, the temperature my sink. During this period, the birds require a protein-rich diet (feathers consist of 88 percent protein). During the molt, they also are more susceptible to bone fractures, due to resorption of calcium from the bone tissue. A bird receiving an inadequate diet occasionally may use its protein-rich new feathers as a supplement!

In ideal conditions, a bird should replace its feathers during the annual molt, without any problems. Occasional problems that may arise during the molt include a bird losing too many feathers at once and having difficulty in replacing them. Such a molt is regarded as abnormal, as is a bird losing feathers outside the normal molting season. In most cases, such abnormal molts occur as a result of extreme environmental factors, for example: unusually high or low temperatures, sudden changes in the weather, shock, disease, or fear. One of the most usual triggers to abnormal molt is

a malfunction of the thyroid gland. Your avian veterinarian will be able to advise you on suggested dietary supplements.

The so-called shock molt, occurs outside the molting season. The bird suddenly starts losing feathers if it is subjected to sudden shock or fear, so great care always should be taken to deal with your birds as gently as possible; especially those that have been acquired recently and are still finding their way around.

Young, immature birds should be left to their own devices as much as possible and allowed *gradually* to become accustomed to their keeper and surroundings. Cats, weasels, mice, rats, owls, and similar should be kept away from your aviaries so that they do not frighten the birds and possibly cause shock molt. I know of many cases of birds contracting shock molt after being caught up at night for treatment for totally different conditions! Tail feathers and smaller body feathers frequently are lost in shock molt, but, remarkably, seldom wing feathers. Tail feather shedding can be compared with autotomy, the involuntary but sometimes voluntary shedding of the tail in many species of lizard. As the bird makes a quiet escape, a predator ends up with a mouthful of tail feathers!

A bird occasionally may develop a permanent molt. This can be caused by a deficiency of certain amino acids in its diet. In such cases, the normal molt also may be incomplete.

Treatment of Abnormal Molt: If the abnormal molt is caused by a diet deficiency, the diet must be revised and corrected. Ensure that plant and animal proteins, and a good vitamin/mineral supplement are contained in the diet. The usual factors appertaining to housing and protection from adverse weather conditions apply. At temperatures below 68° F (20° C) and a relative humidity below 50 percent, a Gouldian finch will stop molting. In the colder months, supplementary heating in the form of ceramic lamps, for example, can be provided. Dull, miserable weather can be brightened for the birds by supplying a supple-

If Your Gouldian Finch Gets Sick

mentary light source. Vita-Lite, for example, is a fluorescent lamp that produces the whole color spectrum of natural sunlight and approximately a similar number of microwatts of ultraviolet per lumen. Additionally, Vita-Lite offers the biological advantages of natural sunlight, something that most kinds of artificial light do not have. A light with the whole color spectrum (especially the ultraviolet part) can have a significant influence on the birds' biological functions, including the production of vitamins in the body and the fixing of calcium in the bone tissues. It scientifically is correct to say that the quality of light has an important influence on the biological functions and, in this respect, I have no hesitation in recommending Vita-Lite as an almost essential acquisition for those who keep their birds indoors, especially during the winter months.

Salmonella

This organism may be responsible for many fatalities in young Gouldians. The rod-like salmonella bacteria cause diarrhea, painful joints, and nervous disorders. Infected birds pass on the bacteria in their droppings or via their saliva (parent birds feeding their young, for example). Salmonella organisms are even able to penetrate the eggshells and affect the embryos.

Salmonella occurs in four forms; all can occur at the same time. *Intestinal form:* The disease organisms attack the walls of the intestines; symptoms include diarrhea, the droppings being foul smelling, slimy, and green or brown (green droppings also can indicate a gall infection—consult a veterinarian immediately). *Joint form:* A strong intestinal infection can result in the bacteria entering the bloodstream and infecting all parts of the body including the bone joints. This causes severe swelling and intense pain, resulting in the bird not using its feet and wings. *Organ form:* Bacteria in the blood can infect any internal organs including the heart, liver, pancreas, kidneys, and other glands, causing gross malfunction of the biologi-

cal processes. The sick bird becomes inactive, mopes in a corner of the cage or aviary, and becomes nearsighted and short of breath. *Nervous form:* Salmonella bacteria infecting the nervous system (brain, spinal chord, and/or nerves) will cause loss of balance, crippling and paralysis, and/or involuntary relaxing of muscles; resulting in such typical symptoms as the awkward turning of the neck, cramp-like contractions of the toes, fouling of the cloaca, and so on.

Should a Gouldian finch become infected with salmonella, serious intestinal problems will develop in just two to three days. The bacteria multiply in the gut linings and eventually gain access to the bloodstream. Young birds, having little or no immunity, quickly succumb to the disease. Older birds however, may incubate the disease over a long period and, if they are not cured adequately, will become carriers capable of infecting other birds via their oviducts or droppings. Heavy losses of young birds during the breeding season are often a sign of salmonellosis in the stock. Consult your vet immediately.

Overgrown Beak and Claws

Beak: It is obvious that the shape and length of the beak are of great importance. A malformed beak will prevent satisfactory feeding and cause difficulties in defense, preening, and feeding the young. A beak that has grown out of shape must thus be trimmed back to its normal shape. A household nail clipper or a pair of sharp nail scissors can be used for this. Take the bird with its back in the palm of your hand and restrain its head gently but firmly between the thumb and forefinger. Carefully trim the beak to shape, taking great care not to cut into the blood vessels. Beginners are advised to obtain instruction from a veterinarian or an experienced breeder before attempting this operation.

Claws: Excessive claw length can cause problems with many bird species, especially finches, including Gouldians. Birds with such a problem

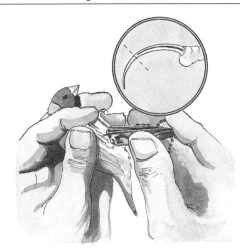

Clipping nails. Avoid the quick, which will bleed if cut.

are in danger of catching on to everything in their accommodation and indirect fatalities are not unknown. Some birds need constant and regular inspection of their nails. A few flagstones or some forest reeds in the aviary will help alleviate the problem. It is quite an easy matter to trim a bird's claws to a reasonable length. Take the bird in the hand with its back laying in the palm and take the leg, near the foot, between middle and forefinger. It is then quite easy to manipulate the foot while cutting the nails with a sharp pair of nail scissors in the other hand. Take great care not to cut into the quick or blood vessel in the claw. In a good light, this can be seen easily showing as a dark line through the horn of the claw. If the blood

vessel is damaged accidentally, use a sterile cotton ball and a styptic agent to stop the bleeding.

Worms

It is very difficult to avoid worm infections of birds in outdoor aviaries. Worm eggs in the droppings of wild birds easily can fall into the aviary.

Roundworms *(Ascaris)*: Ingested eggs hatch into elongated larvae that develop into adult worms in the birds' intestines. These lay eggs that are, in turn, passed out in the droppings. As the worms feed on the partially digested food of the bird, a heavy infection can lead to anemia, weight loss, and general deterioration of condition coupled with diarrhea or constipation. Your veterinarian will be able to identify a positive worm infection from a stool sample. Treatment using piperazine or levamisole usually is successful. First-rate hygiene is the best preventive measure. Try and keep wild birds away from your aviaries, and regular hosing down of concrete floors will remove any infected droppings. A complete change of the topsoil in outdoor flights, about twice per year, also will be a great help.

Threadworms *(Capillaria)*: These are thread-like parasites that reach adulthood in the crop or intestines of a bird. Like roundworms, the threadworms are transmitted by eggs in the feces of infected birds. Diagnosis and treatment is similar to that described for roundworms; prevention also depends on excellent sanitation. To clean floors, use Clorox in a dilution of 6 ounces per gallon of water (a 9 percent solution); this may be corrosive to bare metal.

Understanding Gouldian Finches

The Natural Habitat of the Gouldian Finch

Captive Gouldians kept in conditions that are too cold and damp slowly will pine away, will not come through the molt satisfactorily, and will give deplorable breeding results. That is all not so surprising, when one considers that wild Gouldian finches inhabit the open savannah regions of northern Australia. The most southern limit of their range is roughly at the 19th latitude. Thus the wild habitat of the Gouldian finch is north of this line of latitude, which connects the town of Derby on the northwest coast, with the town of Bowen on the east coast. Unfortunately, the numbers of wild Gouldian finches have declined drastically and still appear to be on the decline. The bird is not found on Cape York Peninsula, probably because the greater part of this area is covered with a subtropical rain forest. One area where it is still reasonably abundant is the Kimberley District in the northwest of the country. The terrain consists of red and brown colored palaeozoic plateaus, divided by deep river gorges. Due to the influence of the northwest monsoon season, coastal areas are mainly mangrove forests, whereas further inland the country is sparsely wooded savannah or grassland.

For the greater part of the year, northern Australia, which is subtropical, is subjected to the southeast trade wind, which originates in the center of the "world's largest island" (as Australia sometimes is called) and is therefore very dry. During the months of November, December, and especially January and February, the area is influenced by the northwest monsoon that pushes through to the 19th latitude and brings a great deal of rainfall. The average annual rainfall at the coast is about 492 inches (1250 cm), whereas the southeastern part of this region receives barely 118 inches (300 cm).

The torrential rains of the rainy season quickly turn the narrow creeks into mighty rivers and large areas of land temporarily are flooded (known affectionately by Australians as "the big wet") forming huge temporary lakes and marshes. The many species of birds that inhabit the area are attracted to these drinking stations. All around, numerous species of plants and grasses grow, some reaching 6 feet (2 m) and more in height. These are an important source of food for the birds.

The sun beats down relentlessly and, it is not for nothing that the Kimberley District frequently is referred to as the "hell" of the southern hemisphere. Maximum temperatures are 104 to 113°F (40-45°C) in the shade and approximately 143°F (62°C) in the full sun. Due to the influence of the sea temperatures, nightly temperature reductions are minimal and, during the rainy season the *lowest* temperature seldom is below 86°F (30°C). The southern part of the region is influenced by the continental climate, and there the lowest temperature during the rainy season is around 60°F (15°C). During the Gouldians' breeding season, the temperatures usually are between 70 and 74°F (22-23°C). During the summer months, the humidity rarely falls below 20 to 30 percent, and during the breeding time of the Goudian finches, this usually is 70 to 80 percent!

A characteristic of the natural habitat of Gouldian finches is the many species of *Eucalyptus* trees, which, with their vertically hanging foliage, provide welcome shade from the harsh rays of the sun. Most of the other species of trees and shrubs in the area shed their leaves in the dry season. The iron-bearing soils of the region support many kinds of grasses, which, as already mentioned, provide seeds for the native finch species.

During the hot weather, the undergrowth dies off giving the finches a chance to find the hard, ripe seeds that are dehusked and eaten on the ground.

It is obvious that two such different seasons with such short changeover periods must place special demands on the life-styles of finches. The Gouldian finch is exceptionally dependent on warmth and, of all Australian finches, is most

Understanding Gouldian Finches

dependent on the sun's rays. It should not surprise you, therefore, to hear that I have observed Gouldian finches at their most active when the sun was a burning ball in the sky. When other bird species seek out the last and smallest patches of shade and sit panting, with their wings outspread, the Gouldians are taking their sunbath!

During the rainy season, the Gouldians are very dependent on the abundant green food and half-ripe seed that they devour with gusto! Both of these conditions cannot always occur together, so the birds must migrate to more suitable areas.

The Three Color Varieties

There are three color morphs of the wild Gouldian finch in Australia *(Chloebia gouldiae)*: the red-headed, the black-headed, and the yellow-headed. All varieties are 5 to 5½ inches (12.5–14 cm) in length, and apart from the spectacular colors, the males are recognized by the long pointed, middle tail feathers that are about 1½ inch (4 cm) long. The tail feathers are shorter in the hens; approximately ¾ to 1 inch (2-2.5 cm).

Although it is a matter of personal preference, I find the red-headed Gouldian finch to be the most attractive of the trio. This bird often is referred to as *Chloebia g. mirabilis.* In the cock bird, the deep-red mask is bordered on the crown by a thin, black band, which broadens on the throat and runs into the black chin. The black band is followed by a light, sky-blue band, which is twice as wide on the crown and sides of the head as it is on the chin.

The breast is lilac or lilac-blue; the remaining underparts, deep-yellow to orange-yellow, running into white around the area of the legs; the under tail coverts are also white; the tibia is a brighter white. The nape, back, and wings are grass-green. The rump and upper tail coverts are light-blue. The tail, and primary wing feathers are black, the latter having green edges; the tail feathers are marked with white dots. The undersides of the wings are silver-gray. The middle, black tail feathers are like needle points. The iride (eye) is dark brown and is surrounded by a thin, lilac, eye ring; the beak is horn-colored with a conspicuous red tip; the legs and feet are pinkish.

The hen is altogether duller in appearance, and usually lacks the blue neckband. The tail is lighter lilac, the underside paler. The red mask is also nowhere near as brightly colored as that of the male. Sometimes, the hens appear to have a black mask, which, if examined closely, will be seen to consist of small red feathers — we can be sure that here we have a genetical red-masked (see page 69).

The second variety is the black-headed Gouldian finch (*Chloebia g. gouldiae*), which is the most abundant variety in the wild. Apart from the black mask, the bird is similarly colored to the above variety.

The hen also has a deep-black head. If small red or yellow feathers can be seen in the mask, we can assume that genetical red-masked is in the makeup. We must not forget to mention here that a homozygote (pure inheriting) black-masked, always has a red tip to the bill; it is possible for a black-masked bird to have a yellow tip to the beak but this will indicate that the bird has the genes of a yellow-masked hen in its makeup (the black melanin hides the yellow in the mask).

The third variety is the yellow-headed Gouldian finch (*Chloebia g. armitiana*), which, in the wild, is very scarce. In the 1960s, these birds were obtained easily in Europe, imported from Japan, where they had been bred extensively. At the present time, the yellow-head is not so abundant as the other varieties. The yellow-headed variety is again similar in color to the other varieties except that it has an orange-red to orange-yellow mask. The hen has a brownish yellow-orange mask, which frequently is intermingled with black feathers.

The colors of juvenile birds are somewhat different. Let us first look at a young Gouldian that has just hatched from the egg. The finch chick is flesh-colored, has no feathers and is thus naked.

Understanding Gouldian Finches

In the angles of the jaw are two blue and one yellow wart-like, light-reflective papillae. On the palate and on the tongue are markings, which, biologically speaking, are characteristic of the species; similar (but not the same) markings are to be found in closely-related finch species, but they are all somewhat different in size and form. In other words, a Gouldian finch does *not* have the same papillae and markings (quantity, color, form, size) as a zebra finch, a blue-faced parrot finch or a diamond firetail finch. They all have their own characteristic papillae and mouth-markings.

In the Gouldian finch there are five black spots on the palate and two on the tongue; two on the inside of the point of the upper mandible and, moreover, a horseshoe-shaped marking on the inside of the lower mandible.

In the dim light of the nest (or of a nest box), these papillae and markings have the function of reflecting the sparse available light and indicating to the parent birds "the way to the crop." When the young birds leave the nest, the papillae and markings are lost respectively from the beak angles, inside the beak, and on the tongue, and disappear when the birds are 2½ to 3 months old.

Before the first molt, juvenile Gouldians are easy to distinguish from adults. They are mainly olive-green above, but with more gray. The upper tail feathers are gray, washed with blue; the edges of the feathers are lighter gray, and easily seen when the wings are closed. Tail and wings are dark-gray with olive green edges. The long, pointed middle tail feathers, are not to be distinguished in length from the other tail feathers. Looking at the head, we will see that the cheeks and forehead are gray to greenish-gray, whereas the chin, throat, most of the belly, and underside of the tail are whitish. The center of the tail is light gray-blue or yellow-gray; in some birds rose-brown, but this color is lighter on the edges, usually light yellowish. The dark eyes are ringed with a featherless, thin, light-blue border. The legs and feet are rose-colored, the beak is horn-colored, sometimes with a little red or yellow. Later in the text we will see how the color on the under mandible will indicate to us whether we have a genetic red-, black-, or yellow-headed Gouldian finch!

It is impossible to distinguish the sexes of the juveniles from the color, but as the cocks begin to try out their vocal cords, first hesitantly, then enthusiastically, we can distinguish them from the silent hens. We do not have to wait long for the cocks to start singing; they will start at 28 to 29 days old or five to seven days after leaving the nest; often all day long providing they are left undisturbed. It is interesting to note that cocks begin their head shaking and bobbing at about 35 days, often accompanied with a beautiful little song. At this point it makes sense to state that newly-emerged youngsters should be left completely in peace for the first few days. If they are disturbed, they may panic and fly around, possibly injuring themselves on the aviary wire or on plants. The birds should be left the first few days to peacefully explore and become accustomed to their surroundings; they will then remain happy and we will have ideal birds! After a few days the young birds will begin to feed themselves and after the second week they will become more or less independent.

Calls

Gouldian finches have various calls for diverse situations. What we describe normally as a "song" sounds like a light and dragging chirp, sometimes trilling, sometimes whispery. This "form" of singing is used by the cock as he courts the hen, but it usually is preceded with a short "sroot" (as in poor); the same call is heard when the cock later tries to attract the hen to the nest; we can therefore call this a "nest call." When the cocks sing "for their own pleasure" (as if practicing) — often observed in young cocks (see page 65) — the nest call is never used, but the song begins with a few trilling notes. The song of the Gouldian finch is very similar to that of many members of the genus *Lonchura* (mannikins and munias).

The Gouldian finch uses the "contact call" more often than what we refer to as the "song." In the wild, it is very easy to hear when a group of birds are moving together; as soon as each bird has perched on a twig it makes this call to others in the neighborhood as if to ensure that all have arrived safely. When the birds perch closely to each other, but without any actual body contact, the contact call is always soft. The contact call is not only heard when the birds sit close to each other on a twig in a tree or tall shrub, but also when they are foraging for food, or gathering at a water hole. Even when the group is in flight, the contact call is uttered continually. In flight, the contact with the partner and the rest of the group is more continuous than when the birds are feeding or drinking. The contact call of the hen is louder than that of the cock. Partners call more urgently than those that are not "committed." Due to the fact that partners always, even in flight, stay close to each other, the contact call is louder and sounds like: "zit zit." If a bird, for one reason or another is separated from the group, or if partners are out of each other's sight, the "lost call" is used; this is loud and sounds like: "zroo eat."

In the breeding season, the birds use the "nest call" both in the nest and when sitting at the nest entrance, so that continual contact is kept between the breeding pair; the call sounds like: "wee-wee-wee-wee-wee." The call also is used when the birds relieve each other for egg brooding. I have several times personally heard cocks in the wild using this call to "order" the hen into the nest. When young are in the nest, after a few days they can be heard calling a continuous "we we we we we." When alarmed, for example, when a predator is spotted, the "alarm call" is a sharp, short "sat sat" (as in bat, act) repeated twice or sometimes three or four times.

Another kind of "warning call" is used when newly-fledged young are in danger; a short, staccato "djit djit" (as in it). As soon as the young are fully grown, they revert to the "sat sat" alarm call.

Courtship

The breeding time of the wild Gouldians is towards the end of the wet season. In contrast to most finch species, Gouldian pairs stay together for a single season; thus both sexes may choose a different partner in the next season. After rearing a few youngsters (up to 20 in a season) the pair will separate.

As soon as the breeding season has begun, the males start to sing in earnest in order to attract the hens. The latter sit nearby on twigs, listening attentively and taking on a special stance (known as *peering*) in which the head is turned in the direction of the singing cock. Sometimes a hen

During the breeding season, the Gouldian finch male starts to sing in earnest. An interested hen will sit nearby on a twig and take a special stance (known as *peering*) in which the head is turned in the direction of the singing male. Sometimes a hen will sit so close to the male that he has to lean to one side. Left hen, right male.

will sit next to a singing cock and hold her head so near to him that he—still singing enthusiastically—has to lean to one side.

Pair Formation

The male performs a somewhat comical courtship display for the benefit of the hen (see page 33). The performance usually occurs on a horizontal branch. He twists and turns in all manner of positions in order to show all his colors off to his intended partner.

The display falls into two phases. In the first phase, the cock takes a slanting posture on the twig, *partly* fluffing out his face feathers and *fully* fluffing out the feathers of the nape. The breast and belly feathers are also puffed out so that the purple areas of the upper body appear larger, in the hope of impressing his future spouse. At the same time, he directs his tail in her direction. Next, he begins the so-called "beak wiping," whereby the cock moves his beak very quickly along and over the twig, but without actually touching it.

In the second phase of the courtship ritual, the male stretches out to his full length and holds his head (and thus also his beak) in the direction of his purple breast while making little jumps by bending and stretching his feet—but without significantly altering his position. All this time he will be singing at the top of his voice and holding his tail in the direction of the hen. A receptive hen will respond by holding her tail in the direction of her suitor. Both phases of the ritual may be performed several times. If the hen is not interested in the male's approaches, she will show it in her manner; although she may watch indifferently, she will not further react and thus will not respond with her tail and will not go and sit close to the dancing cock. After a while, the cock will stop performing to the disinterested hen and go off in search of another partner. Should the female genuinely be interested in the male's performances, she will stay close to him, twisting her tail in his direction and making shaking movements of the feathers. Frequently she also will make nodding

The first courtship display phase: The cock takes an oblique (slanting) posture on a twig, *partly* fluffing out his face feathers and *fully* fluffing out the feathers on the back of the head. He then twists his tail in the direction of the hen, and puffs out the feathers of the breast and belly, so that the purple areas appear larger and more impressive.

The second courtship display phase: The male stretches out to his full length and hold his beak in the direction of the breast while making little jumps. An interested female will make nodding movements with the head.

The second courtship display phase (continued): Further bobbing (nodding) of the head by the male.

The second courtship display phase (continued): A receptive female will respond to the advances of the male by holding her tail in the direction of her suitor.

movements with the head, similar to those made by the male, though not quite so enthusiastically. The positive reaction from the hen will make the male even more enthusiastic in his singing and dancing, with his beak almost laid upon his breast and slowly moving it back and forth. There are possible variations to this behavior; the interested hen, for example, may turn her upper body towards the cock so that the two are sitting opposite and parallel to each other on the perch. She will puff out her body feathers, after which the male usually flies to the nest. If not immediately followed by the hen, then he returns to the perch and begins the whole performance once again.

Nest Building

After the first rains of the season, the vegetation will grow prolifically and an abundance of half-ripe seeds will become available. At this time, many flying insects such as termites, flies, beetles, and also spiders are available and these all become part of the menu (see page 29).

Now that such an abundance of easily obtainable food is available, the Gouldians begin to build their nests. There are also plenty of water holes, which are visited usually but once per day, in the early mornings. The drinking method is unique; the birds suck up the water, which is made possible by the peristaltic movements of the esophagus (tube connecting the mouth with the stomach).

Freely-suspended nests rarely are constructed; as hole brooders, the Gouldians seek out, for example, abandoned nests of kingfishers or parakeets, hollow limbs, hollows in termite mounds, and so on. The nursery usually is constructed with sparse materials; indeed, I have found nests with no nest material at all, the eggs having been deposited and brooded on the natural lining of the cavity. Occasionally, a nest is constructed on a forked branch, but this seems to account for fewer than 25 percent of the total nests. These nests are so sparsely constructed that one frequently can see the brooding bird through the nest material! In ideal conditions, the birds will rear two or three broods per season.

In the wild, several pairs often may nest close to each other in the same hollow limb or termite mound. It is usually the males that seek out the nest sites. Possible sites are carefully and cautiously inspected (especially as snakes and other predators are common in the Gouldians' habitat). Once he has found a suitable spot for nest building, he will let out his enthusiastic nest calls so that the hen also will come and inspect. If acceptable, the cock will then begin to gather nesting materials. In most cases, pairing takes place in the nest.

Eggs

Once the nest is constructed, the hen begins to lay. The first egg usually is laid early in the morning; and a further egg each day thereafter to a total of four to nine. The eggs are white in color. Ornithologists are not yet quite agreed on when brooding begins, but it is suspected it starts before the last egg is laid. This means, of course, that youngsters hatch at different times. Sometimes it can be three days between the first and the last egg hatching.

Incubation

The hen does most of the brooding; she sits all night, but during the day the cock will relieve her regularly. In this period, both birds have "brood patches"; areas of bare skin full of blood vessels that come in direct contact with the eggs.

As the day temperature frequently is very high, it can happen that brooding is not continuous. The chances of sudden cooling are remote. The breeding birds thus have a chance for social gathering (see page 65).

The "changing of the guard" takes place inside the nest; the bird doing the relieving emits continuous nest calls so that the brooding bird is warned and does not receive a shock.

With regard to intruders (see page 35): if unwelcome guests (frequently other Gouldians) get too close for comfort, the birds have a special threat behavior. The body is lowered so it comes almost in contact with the perch and the head is stretched forward. If the intruder does not depart

quickly, the defender will make head movements similar to a bird begging for food. In this behavior, the intruder is looked sharply in the eye and all sorts of head movements are made. I personally find that the hen is more intensive in this behavior than the cock. Should a predator visit the nest, defense is usually "out of the question" and the brooding bird will flee. The aviculturist Van der Mark says that the influence of fear is greater than the will to defend. It is possible that this fear is a subconscious, inherited defense against the (very real) possibility of a snake entering the nest.

Young

After a couple of weeks, the eggs will hatch and the young are fed on regurgitated food. Due to the mouth, tongue, beak markings, and the luminous nodules (see page 37), the parent birds easily can see where to place the food. In addition, the hatchlings emit their begging calls and hold their heads high. At 10–12 days old and after they have left the nest, the head is more or less held back between the shoulders, while the neck is turned sideways with the beak held upwards.

Newly-hatched young are completely naked; the skin is pink in color. The eyes open after about seven days; after 11–12 days the first primary feathers appear. The young leave the nest at 20–22 days of age; in the wild this sometimes may be a little older and will depend on things like bad weather (rain) when the parents have a more difficult time to find adequate food. Having left the nest, the fledglings never return, even to spend the night, although — especially in the first week — they will stay fairly close to it. This makes it easier for the parents to find them and continue to feed them. At about 35 days of age the young can

Above left: A yellow-headed dilute-bodied male; ▶ Above right: A blue-bodied male with buff abdomen. In this mutation, the color yellow is almost entirely eliminated, leaving the color blue. Below: The rare silver hen, a mutation that was first bred in the Netherlands.

Understanding Gouldian Finches

Gouldian nestlings showing their markings.

be regarded as independent. It regularly can happen that, in ideal conditions, the first brood of the season can itself rear a brood before that current season is over — these young parents are thus seldom over two months old!

Molt

The molt usually starts after the end of the breeding season. The youngsters go through their first molt at six to eight weeks, but this sometimes can take several months before it totally is completed. The new feathers come first in the area of the belly, then on the rump; these are followed by those on the head and breast, then the back and wings. The central tail feathers come last.

Social Behavior

During the dry season, Gouldian finches often gather in large flocks; in some years there are

◀ Above: yellow-headed yellow-bodied hen. Below: Gouldian finches love spray millet, and will peck and pry into the stalks for hours! Seed alone, however, will bring nutritional problems. Therefore, always include high protein foodstuffs in your bird's diet.

reports of groups of a thousand or more assembling. Due to illegal trapping, smuggling, agriculture, cattle farming (overgrazing), mining (iron ore and diamonds), and spreading of air sac mites (see page 47), the wild Gouldian finch population is alarmingly on the decline.

Most birds are seen by the water holes, often accompanying other species of grass finch (Bicheno, crimson, long-tailed, masked, zebra, and others), various cockatoos (especially Galahs), budgerigars (parakeets), bustards, kookaburras, and goshawks. The goshawk is one of the most active predators of Gouldians and the latter (and other small bird species) especially are cautious when they go to drink. They never spend a long time slaking their thirst but after a few seconds will fly into the air to inspect the area for signs of danger. If all is clear, they then return to the water and drink for a few seconds before repeating the process. At the first threatening sign, they disperse.

Due to their bright colors, Gouldians are spotted easily by predators — in which I will include snakes and egg- and chick-eating mammals (including the feral cat). In larger groups the birds are safer as many eyes are more likely to spot danger! If a bird is attacked by a predator, the flock often will seek out another water hole.

After the start of the wet season, the flocks break up into smaller groups. In the late afternoon, the birds from these groups can be seen together. With their contact calls (see page 59), the birds stay together and go drinking and bathing. On return, they sit by each other on their perches. Body contact is seldom part of their social behavior and the birds always preen themselves. However, the older birds usually sing at these "social gatherings" and the youngsters listen attentively before attempting to imitate them.

The Development of Gouldian Aviculture

John Gould spent the years 1838–1840 in Australia accompanied by his artist wife, and the result was many beautiful illustrations. Alas, she died on their return to England (in 1841). In honor of her work and her help, Gould named the most beautiful finch in the world after her: Lady Gouldian Finch *(Amandina gouldiae)*.

The first bird seen and described by Gould was a black-headed specimen, which had been shot in the vicinity of the Victoria River. A short time after this, Gould received two youngsters from a Mr. Gilbert who had found them near Port Essington (1840). But it was not until 1887 that the first red-headed and black-headed Gouldian finches were imported into Europe. The extremely rare yellow-headed variety was not seen in Europe until 1915.

Around the turn of the century aviculturists began to experiment with the captive breeding of these beautiful birds. In 1888 Dr. E.P. Ramsay bred them in the aviaries of the Australian Museum in Sydney. In 1891, the first successful English breeder was Reginald Phillips. Perhaps Phillips's inexperience with the birds led to his successes and over the years he was able to interbreed with different head color varieties. But in general, Gouldians were not particularly easy birds to breed — many fanciers even had a hard job keeping the birds alive for more than a couple months!

It was the English aviculturist P.W. Teague who, as far as we know, was the first to build, from two pairs of birds, an unbroken stud of 24 generations of Gouldians during the years 1930–1946. Teague was very exact in his work and he wrote his observations and experiences in detail in the (British) *Avicultural Magazine*. It is understandable that his articles are used by many fanciers as guidelines. Indeed, one can agree that most of what Teague wrote is still correct today! Teague had the fortune to live in the southwest coast of England, where the Gulf Stream promotes a relatively mild climate. He kept his birds in outdoor aviaries (but with well-insulated night shelters). During the winter, the birds were kept in timber sheds where they were sheltered from drafts and dampness. Alas, many fanciers elsewhere in England and also on the continent, thought that Teague's methods were correct, whatever the prevailing climate. This led to the premature deaths of many birds that could not acclimate to the inclement weather. Teague had started his hobby with strong birds, directly imported from Australia. Of course, other fanciers in England and Europe had access to similar birds but their breeding results were nowhere near as successful as Teague's. The Second World War led to a break in progress.

It was many years before imported Gouldians were again available but, in the fifties, imports began to grow to massive proportions. Australia saw, rightly so, that such massive captures of wild birds posed a danger to their continued existence and, in 1960 legislation was passed preventing the further export of the birds. After 1960 it was still possible to obtain birds from the breeding aviaries of Japan, often birds that were raised by society finch foster parents (see page 43). In general, the quality of these birds was mediocre to bad.

With regard to the breeding of Gouldians, Teague used a biologically well thought-out system. He allowed a pair of Gouldians to raise its family in an outdoor aviary — if there were two or three broods this did not matter — the younger and older birds and their parents were all left together in a group. Thus, at the end of the breeding season, he had the original breeding pair with the young from two or three broods.

The social contact that occurred throughout the breeding season was continued later as the birds were kept together in a large family group. It was thus possible for Teague to study the birds and, in due time, to select those most suitable for further pairing. Such a technique is recommended highly to breeders today, although it is accepted that not all fanciers have as much time to spend with their birds as Teague. However Teague's years of experimentation has given us at least techniques for which we should be thankful.

The Genetics of Gouldian Finches

The Body's Building Blocks

Of all the myriads of higher life forms, each is derived from the merger of an egg cell provided by the mother, and a sperm cell contributed by the father. The penetration of the egg cell by the sperm results in a new cell being formed, the *zygote,* which, over a period of time, develops into a new living being. By applying this knowledge to Gouldian finches, we know that when a cock and hen Gouldian mate, the former is fertilizing the eggs of the latter with his sperm. Each of the resulting mergers will develop into a fertile egg containing a developing Gouldian embryo, which, if all goes well, eventually will be an adult Gouldian that will be able to perform the same functions as its parents.

The bodies of all higher beings, whether man, beast, bird, or plant, are made up from millions of minute cells, all of which are derived from a single starter cell by means of *cell division.* In such division of the cell, both the cytoplasm (protoplasm excluding the nucleus) and nucleus (body containing the chromosomes) divide into two individual cells by constriction. In this manner, one cell becomes two; two cells give rise to four; four cells develop into eight — and so on. With just ten such divisions we already have 1,024 cells. Once underway, cell division can be very fast.

The contents of the egg therefore develop by cell division. The zygote (or starter cell) forms the egg yolk, which is surrounded by a layer of albumin (egg white) and further protected by the egg shell. Each individual egg lies in the nest waiting to be brooded until, 15 days later a young Gouldian will hatch. Cell division progresses thereafter until the bird reaches adulthood, and indeed continues throughout its life (at a diminished rate) for the repair and maintenance of body tissues (injury, molt, and so on).

To delve deeper into the subject, let us return to the original egg cell and sperm cell. These are called *gametes* or reproductive cells. A male gamete and a female gamete together contain everything that contributes to the development of a new bird. Once united, the gametes give rise to a new body, wings, feathers, eyes, color, and so on.

Chromosomes

Inside the united gametes (the zygote), the whole miracle of reproduction takes place. In that small space, the carriers of life organize the manufacture of a new bird. These carriers of life are called *chromosomes* and they are contained in the nucleus of the cells. As mentioned above, the zygote develops by division into two, four, eight cells — and so on. If this process were to go on for too long, we would end up with a Gouldian finch the size of a horse! There has to be a controlling mechanism, which, at the right moment, says: "Halt! Development is complete. We must now concentrate on maintenance."

This mechanism is provided by the chromosomes, which, under the microscope, can be seen inside the cell nucleus. The chromosomes contain some smaller bodies called *genes,* which determine the genetic traits of the developing bird. They are responsible for every detail in the new Gouldian, including color and shape. What the individual genes influence is very important to the serious breeder of Gouldians.

Each cell in the body contains a certain number of chromosomes — always in even numbers. When a cell divides, the chromosomes also divide so that each new cell contains the same numbers of chromosomes as the parent cell. If, for example, the original cell contains eight chromosomes then, after division, each of the two new cells also will have eight chromosomes. Normal cells always have the same number of chromosomes and, no matter how many times division occurs, the daughter cells will maintain eight chromosomes.

Reproductive Cells: An Exception

Reproductive cells represent an exception to the basic rule of cell division. The egg cell and the

The Genetics of Gouldian Finches

sperm cell contain half the usual number of chromosomes. For example, Gouldian finches have 14 chromosomes in their normal body cells, but the female egg cell and the male sperm cell contain only seven each. Thus, during fertilization, the two sets of seven meld to form a zygote with 14 chromosomes. Further division however results in every new cell having 14 chromosomes.

Why does this happen? There is a reason for everything in nature. If the egg cell and the sperm cell each contained the normal number of Gouldian chromosomes (14), then a resulting zygote would contain 28 chromosomes, giving rise to a "Gouldian" with body cells of 28 chromosomes. In fact, it could not be a Gouldian at all as it would not have the proper number of chromosomes in its cells to be one!

Such reflections are academic however. By the rules of heredity, both the egg cell and the sperm cell must have half the number of ordinary cell chromosomes so that together they form a zygote with half the traits of each parent. Because chromosomes are carriers of the various hereditary traits transmitted by the genes, the bird inherits traits from both parents according to their own genetic makeup.

No Watercolor Set

If, for example, one parent bird were white and the other green, the young would inherit both white and green color genes. One would expect the young, therefore, to look more or less half green and half white, or some color in between. But Nature does not work like a watercolor set that makes light green by mixing green and white together. There are more elements that influence heredity.

There are visible and invisible genetic factors called *dominant* and *recessive*. If you dislike technical terms, you could call them *aggressive factors* and *shy factors*. These are of prime importance in the hereditary of Gouldian finches. In most cases, one color factor is dominant.

A red-headed Gouldian male, for example, can be black-headed at the same time, even though the black is invisible, for it is overpowered by the red color. In other words, the red color is dominant to the black and the bird is known as "dominant red" or, if you like, "recessive black," the bird having inherited the black gene from one of its parents, even though it is not visible.

Homozygous versus Heterozygous

A bird with no hidden color traits is a *homozygote,* which could be translated as *inheriting purely,* whereas a bird that carries a hidden color trait, as discussed above, is referred to as a *heterozygote* or *inheriting impurely.* A homozygous and a heterozygous bird can therefore look exactly alike. However, a homozygous (or purely inheriting) red-headed Gouldian is purely red-headed in its makeup, whereas a heterozygous red-headed bird can look just as red-headed but carries a hidden, invisible trait for another color.

Unfortunately, many Gouldian finch fanciers breed their birds in cages and aviaries in the colony system. This makes record keeping extremely difficult and the consequence is that little or nothing is known about the heritage of their birds. Only breeders who keep to "one pair per cage" for several seasons will be sure what type of birds they are dealing with. Only then can they profess to supply genetically pure breeding stock (for color), and to be producing successful lineages.

When geneticists speak of red-headed, black-headed, white-breasted, blue-backed, and so on, they always refer to the pure color—the color of homozygous birds. If a bird is heterozygous, they indicate this by recording the invisible color after the visible one. For example, a red-headed bird that also carries a black-headed factor is called red-headed/black-headed. When read out loud, this is sounded as "red-headed split for black-headed," and the bird could be called "black-headed blooded."

By now, you will understand that someone

The Genetics of Gouldian Finches

who buys a pair of Gouldian finches without a forethought, will never be sure how the young will turn out. You cannot just go by looks, because you might be dealing with either homozygous or heterozygous birds, or one of each. In most cases, the haphazard buyer will get heterozygotes — impure birds — because most breeders understand too little about the theory of color inheritance. They breed shotgun style under the motto, "Whatever will be, will be."

Serious breeders attain a good understanding of the colors lurking in their stock after a few matings. If you know what is hidden inside your birds, then you accurately and easily can predict the result of any crossing.

Red-headed Gouldian Finch

We know that Gouldian finches occur in the wild in three head-colors: red, black, and orange (usually referred to as yellow). The black and yellow colorations are regarded as head color *mutations*, whereas the red-headed is regarded as *normal*. The red color may appear in various degrees of clarity, depending upon the availability of sunlight and suitable humidity. As sunlight and humidity are not constant in the various kinds of wild habitat, the red-color on wild birds also may vary somewhat. If the advice of this book is followed, and a uniform temperature and humidity are provided, there may still be a variance in the clarity of the red color. The young usually will inherit a particular shade of red from one of their parents; in other words, the red color is controlled genetically.

A mature cock always will have a fully red mask, with no trace of black feathers. The hens however seldom have an unblemished mask, and it usually is sprinkled with a number of dark feathers. Sometimes indeed there are so many black feathers that it is difficult to spot any red ones! I once had a red-headed hen, which, in her first year, showed not the slightest trace of a red feather, so that I thought it was a black-headed speci-

men. I mated her with a black-headed cock and was somewhat amazed to see that all the young from the first brood were red-headed! She surprised me again in the following season, when, after the molt, she developed a beautiful red mask with scarcely a black feather in sight! Over the years, I have noted that the mask of hens frequently gets redder after each molt until, after two or three years, they possess a deep red mask without a single black feather!

The belief that red-headed Gouldians with black feathers in their masks are crosses between red- and black-headed types is false. Red-headed hens, even those with hardly any red in the mask at first, are genetically red-headed Gouldians.

Red-heads are dominant over the black and the yellow (orange) forms. Red-headed cocks can be split for black-headed, but hens can never be so; they only inherit the color seen in the mask. In other words, the hens are homozygous. Such inheritance is known as a *sex-linked inheritance*. The gene for red-headed hens is attached to the

TABLE I

Matings list of Red-headed (RH) and Black-headed (BH) Gouldian Finches in all combinations	
1. RH male (homozygous*) × RH hen	= 50% RH males (homozygous) 50% RH hen
2. RH male (heterozygous**) × H hen	= 25% RH males (homozygous) 25% RH males (heterozygous) 25% RH hens 25% BH hens
3. RH male (homozygous) × H hen	= 50% RH males (heterozygous) 50% RH hens
4. RH male (heterozygous) × H hen	= 25% RH males (heterozygous) 25% BH males 25% RH hens 25% BH hens
5. BH male × RH hen	= 50% RH males (heterozygous) 50% BH hens
6. BH male × BH hen	= 50% BH males 50% BH hens
*A bird without hidden color traits: inheriting purely. **A bird with one or more hidden color traits in addition to its apparent color: inheriting impurely.	

The Genetics of Gouldian Finches

sex-chromosome and so the inheritance is sex-linked.

Table I (see page 69) shows the results of sex-linked inheritance between red-headed and black-headed Gouldians. The percentages given here will not necessarily be true from the beginning. A large number of broods will be necessary before these theoretical figures will be realized.

Black-headed Gouldian Finch

We have mentioned already that, in the wild, black-headed Gouldians outnumber the red-headed, dominant form (in a ratio of about three to one). This is because homozygous birds inherit black, whereas the red-headed can be split for black and thus inherit black. It is then not so surprising that, in our captive birds, more black-headed individuals occur than red-headed. If we do not take special care in our breeding strategies, we therefore will produce large numbers of black-headed hens. Examine Table I once more; a black-headed male paired with a red-headed hen will produce only black-headed females. A red-headed male, split for black (red-headed/black-headed) × a red-headed hen theoretically will produce 25 percent black-headed hens.

Young black-headed males can be expected from two crossings, namely black × black, and red-headed (male) × black-headed (female); in the latter pairing the male has to be split for black (red-headed/black-headed).

Research has shown that black-headed males and red-headed/black-headed males are the most virile, not only in the wild but also in captivity, producing large numbers of young and having a relatively long life.

Yellow (orange)-headed Gouldian Finch

This rare (in the wild) variety (one yellow to approximately 3000 black- and red-headed Gouldians) thankfully is bred quite regularly in captiv-

ity. The yellow mask is inherited recessively as, with the large numbers in the wild, the chances of two yellow-heads mating are much smaller than say yellow × black or yellow × red.

In cage or aviary, however we can choose to pair yellow × yellow. Split yellows do occur, but these outwardly are not distinguishable from reds or blacks. Table II (see page 71) gives the results expected from pairings with yellow-headed birds.

As with red-headed Gouldians, the yellow can be very variable in intensity; it ranges from orange-red to light yellow in males, and from brownish yellow-orange to medium yellow in the hens. In the latter case, many black feathers may be present, as is the case with red-headed Gouldian hens.

The recessive inheritance in yellow-headed Gouldians is, in fact, a "loss-mutation." The birds are not capable of converting the yellow carotene (any of three isomeric red hydrocarbons found in many plants, especially carrots, and transformed to vitamin A in the liver) into red. If we analyze the fat-color in the feather of a red-headed male, we will find pure astaxanthin, whereas that from a yellow-headed male will produce mainly lutein. In this respect, it is interesting to note that the stunning colors of a Gouldian's feathers are due entirely to structural blue, and four color pigments: eumelanin (black), phaeomelanin (reddish-brown), astaxanthin (red), and lutein (yellow). We now know that lutein is not manufactured in the body but is absorbed from foodstuffs, whereas astaxanthin is manufactured from lutein.

To return to our yellow-headed Gouldians: as we know, a yellow-head will have a yellow tip to the beak. Thus the inability to produce red coloring does not apply only to the mask color, but to the whole body, especially in the beak tip.

If we examine Table II, we will see that red-headed hens and cocks can be split for yellow — a property bonded with the recessive inheritance of the yellow-headed Gouldian finch.

The Genetics of Gouldian Finches

TABLE II

Matings list of Yellow-headed (YH) and Red-headed (RH) Gouldian Finches	
1. RH (male or hen, homozygous) × RH (male or hen, heterozygous)	= 50% RH (males or hens, heterozygous) 50% RH (males or hens, homozygous)
2. RH (male, heterozygous) × RH (hen, heterozygous)	= 25% YH (males or hens) 50% RH (males or hens, heterozygous) 25% RH (males or hens, homozygous)
3. YH (male or hen) × RH (male or hen, homozygous)	= 100% RH (males or hens, heterozygous)
4. YH (male or hen) × RH (male or hen, heterozygous)	= 50% YH (males or hens) 50% RH (males or hens, heterozygous)
5. YH (male) × YH (hen)	= 50% YH (males) 50% YH (hens)

An interesting case involves the black-headed Gouldian with a yellow tip to the beak. Do not imagine that this is a black-headed Gouldian split for yellow mask! This bird is really genetically a yellow-mask and is incapable of building red color or or suppressing the black that hides the yellow. The foregoing discussion leads us to the conclusion that a normal black-headed finch with a red-tipped beak, is dominant over the yellow-mask; the same applies for a black-mask with a yellow-tipped beak! We therefore do not have split birds — they are all genetically yellow-masked.

Unfortunately we do not yet know precisely how the inheritance works. The biologist Horst Bielfeld produced the following results from pairing many yellow-beaked black masks with yellow masks: about 75 percent yellow-beaked black masks and 25 percent yellow-masks.

White-breasted Gouldian Finch

In 1967, F. Barnicoat wrote, in *Avicultural Magazine,* an interesting and informative article about a most beautiful mutation: the white-breasted Gouldian finch.

At the present time, this mutation is quite common in our cages and aviaries; the literature indicates that it was known in Australia in 1954 and in South Africa in the late 1950s but it had been difficult to establish. In January 1965, Barnicoat obtained two white-breasted males from a bird dealer in Johannesburg (South Africa) and was able to build up an excellent strain of white-breasted Gouldians in all three head colors. The birds have a pure white chest-band instead of a purple one.

This mutation is inherited recessively, and it is possible to breed in all three mask colors. The birds seem to remain virile and ''brood-happy,'' but there unfortunately are certain negative factors. The hens are used far too often as ''egg producing machines'' and the chicks are reared by society finches, producing birds of an inferior quality. It is therefore the responsiblity of us breeders to obtain fit and healthy birds reared by their own parents and not by foster parents.

As the mutation is recessive, we naturally will expect there to be normal looking birds split for white-breasted, in addition to white-breasted birds with the three head colors. A pairing particularly recommended is split white-breasted × white-breasted, which produces strong, lively offspring.

Experience has shown that white-breasted × white-breasted produces smaller, weaker birds. I therefore make it a rule to pair a normal, virile bird with a white-breasted individual. For further expectations, see Table III (page 72).

The Genetics of Gouldian Finches

TABLE III

Matings list of White-breasted with Normal (= the "wild"-colored red-, black-, and yellow-headed Gouldians, with the purple breast patch)	
1. Normal male (homozygous) × Normal hen (heterozygous)	= 50% Normal (homozygous) 50% Normal (heterozygous)
2. Normal male (heterozygous) × Normal hen (heterozygous)	= 25% White-breasted 50% Normal (heterozygous) 25% Normal (homozygous)
3. White-breasted male × Normal hen (homozygous)	= 100% Normal (heterozygous)
4. White-breasted male × Normal hen (heterozygous)	= 50% White-breasted 50% Normal (heterozygous)
5. White-breasted male × White-breasted hen	= 100% White breasted

Lilac- or Rose-breasted Gouldian Finch

These brilliant birds first appeared in the late 1970s. The males have a lilac, rather than purple chest-band. The mutation arose from crossings of split white-breasted × split white-breasted, and split white-breasted × white-breasted. The mutation is possible in all three head colors.

Experiments have shown that this mutation is dominant to white-breasted, and recessive to the three normal or purple-breasted finches. Lilac-breasted × normal therefore gives normal split for lilac-breasted.

Research by Professor M. Pomarede (published in *Le Journal des Oiseaux*, April, 1983) indicates that the lilac-breasted mutation is derived from the black pigment (eumelanin) in the breast feathers being deficient, hence the red-brown pigment (phaeomelanin) remains. The breast of the male becomes thus old-rose, that of the hen a lighter lilac color. It is interesting to comment at this stage about the plumage colors in the three normal colored Gouldian finches. Firstly, it must be stated that Gouldians do not manufacture the blue color in the body; it is a structural color. The simplest form of structure color is the pigment-free (white) color. The light rays falling upon it are reflected wholly, in other words, there is no light absorption. The reflection of the light occurs in the barbs of the feathers, which contain arbitrary rows of spongelike, hollow cylinders. Along this structure, light rays are reflected in particular densities, giving an impression of colors. Other examples are the structural colors of humming birds and starlings. In Gouldians, the reflected color is blue.

The four pigment colors in the feathers of normal Gouldian finches are:
• Two melanins, eumelanin or black, and phaeomelanin or reddish-brown:
• Two carotenoids, lutein or yellow, and astaxantin or red (see page 70).

The breast thus contains eumelanin and phaeomelanin, the latter making the strong structural blue color into lilac. As there usually is less black eumelanin in the breast feathers of females, the lilac color is lighter. However, there are also greater color variations in the hens than in the cocks. I have seen hens with a breast the color of red wood, and also hens with breasts hardly distinguishable from those of the males! It seems that the eumelanin can occur in various densities.

Blue-breasted Gouldian Finch

The first blue-breasted Gouldian finches appeared around the mid 1970s. This mutation, which is dominant to the three normals, is greatly appreciated in the United States, but many breeders in Europe, South Africa, and Australia also are dedicated to it. Nevertheless, it is not an easy mutation to breed and maintain. The cocks have a medium blue breast, whereas in the hens, this is a soft or light blue.

I personally believe that the blue-breasted is not a real mutation, and agree with Professor Pomarede (in: *Journal des Oiseaux*, April 1983) that this is an over-melanization of the plumage, in which the colors darken and in parts become black. Prof. Pomarede gives a useful summary:
• Purple-breasted: black melanin (eumelanin) and red melanin (phaeomelanin) both present.

The Genetics of Gouldian Finches

- Blue-breasted: red melanin absent.
- Lilac-breasted: only red melanin present.
- White-breasted: all melanin absent.

Blue Gouldian Finch

The mutation that originated in Australia in the 1960s never appeared in Europe or America, due to Australia's tough export regulations. However, independent European strains of the mutation have been developed since the 1970s.

The birds possess dark turquoise wings, back, shoulders, neck, and back of head; the hens are lighter in color than the cocks. With black-headed birds the mask color is barely or totally unchanged, but with red-headed birds the mask is pale yellowish-brown. In all birds the feet and beak are light horn-colored; the red or yellow beak tip is absent. The underside of the body is light-cream instead of yellow.

This color description indicates that the fat color (lipochrome) is absent. The bird is unable to absorb the carotene out of its foodstuff and into its plumage. This can be seen clearly on the red-head, in which the red color is replaced by yellowish-brown depending on the amount of brownish phaeomelanin and yellowish-brown eumelanin. In the belly area, the phaeomelanin itself appears to have acquired a yellowish character (replacing the white) forming the cream color. Due to the absence of the yellow fat color, the pigment lutein, the back and wings are "colored" with the structural color blue.

This mutation is inherited recessively to the three normals. There are thus normal Gouldians that are split for blue. These split birds can sometimes be recognized in appearance in that they may possess a sprinkling of blue feathers.

It is possible to breed blue into the blue-breasted, lilac-breasted, and white-breasted. It is even possible to breed white Gouldians with the blue mutation, by pairing blue to yellow. In the second generation one can then expect to produce blue, yellow (lutino), normal ("wild" colors), and white. The normals can be split or homozygous.

Yellow or Lutino Gouldian Finch

The most important feature of this mutation is that the birds do not have the ability to manufacture melanins (eumelanin and phaeomelanin). Therefore eye pigment is lacking, giving them the appearance of being red. Red (astaxantin), yellow (lutein), and white remain. The lutino occurs in red-headed and yellow-headed forms. These are beautiful birds: yellow with a red mask!

Although the first examples of this mutation appeared in Australia in the 1960s, we can thank the Dutch breeder, G. Megens, that the strain is now well established.

White or Albino Gouldian Finch

This mutation also first appeared in Australia in the 1960s. The birds lack melanins, lipochromes, and pigments (yellow to red). The eye pigment also is absent, giving the eyes a red color (caused by the visible blood vessels). I have seen good white colored birds in the Netherlands with dark eyes. The birds had a little yellow in the feathers of the breast, in the mask and tip of the beak. The upper side of the body and wings were tinted with cream.

These birds also originated from the stud of G. Megens, but the exact genetical explanation is yet to be discovered. It has been concluded that crossings of lutinos with pastel colors can lead to white offspring (in pastel birds, there is general dilution of colors, a phenomenon occuring now and again in all three normal colors).

Dilute-backed Gouldian Finch

The birds from this mutation have a deficiency of pigment, so that the melanin in the wing and back feathers is reduced dramatically. As the structural blue color cannot be produced, the color becomes yellowish or greenish-yellow. In the normal black-masked, the head becomes grayish; in red and yellow masks, the colors stay more or less unchanged.

Matings List (54 possible matings)

Head and Beak Color Variations
(Parents: male × female; offspring (percent))

1. *Yellow-headed × Red-headed*
50% Red-headed/Yellow-headed males
50% Red-headed/Yellow-headed females

2. *Yellow-headed × Red-headed/Yellow-headed*
25% Red-headed/Yellow-headed males
25% Yellow-headed males
25% Red-headed/Yellow-headed females
25% Yellow-headed females

3. *Yellow-headed × Yellow-headed*
50% Yellow-headed males
50% Yellow-headed females

4. *Yellow-headed × Black-headed*
50% Red-headed/Black-headed and Yellow-headed males
50% Red-headed/Yellow-headed females

5. *Yellow-headed × Black-headed/Yellow-headed*
25% Red-headed/Black-headed and Yellow-headed males
25% Yellow-headed/Black-headed males
25% Red-headed/Yellow-headed females
25% Yellow-headed females

6. *Yellow-headed × Black-headed with yellow bill*
50% Yellow-headed/Black-headed males
50% Yellow females

7. *Yellow-headed/Black-headed × Red-headed*
25% Red-headed/Yellow-headed males
25% Red-headed/Black-headed and Yellow-headed males
25% Red-headed/Yellow-headed females
25% Black-headed/Yellow-headed females

8. *Yellow-headed/Black-headed × Red-headed/Yellow-headed*
12½% Red-headed/Yellow-headed males
12½% Yellow-headed males
12½% Yellow-headed/Black-headed males
12½% Red-headed/Black-headed and Yellow-headed males
12½% Red-headed/Yellow-headed females
12½% Yellow-headed females
12½% Black-headed/Yellow-headed females
12½% Black-headed/Black-headed with yellow bill females

9. *Yellow-headed/Black-headed × Yellow-headed*
25% Yellow-headed/Black-headed males
25% Yellow-headed males
25% Yellow-headed females
25% Black-headed/Black-headed with yellow bill

10. *Yellow-headed/Black-headed × Black-headed*
25% Red-headed/Black-headed and Yellow-headed males
25% Black-headed/Yellow-headed males
25% Red-headed/Yellow-headed females
25% Black-headed/Yellow-headed females

11. *Yellow-headed/Black-headed × Black-headed/Yellow-headed*
12½% Red-headed/Black-headed and Yellow-headed males
12½% Yellow-headed/Black-headed males
12½% Black-headed/Yellow-headed males
12½% Black-headed/Black-headed with yellow bill
12½% Red-headed/Yellow-headed females
12½% Yellow-headed females
12½% Black-headed/Yellow-headed females
12½% Black-headed/Black-headed with yellow bill females

12. *Yellow-headed/Black-headed × Black-headed with yellow bill*
25% Yellow-headed/Black-headed males
25% Black-headed with yellow bill males
25% Yellow-headed females
25% Black-headed with yellow bill females

13. *Black-headed × Red-headed*
50% Red-headed/Black-headed males
50% Black-headed females

14. *Black-headed × Red-headed/Yellow-headed*
25% Red-headed/Black-headed males
25% Red-headed/Black-headed and Yellow-headed males
25% Black-headed/Yellow-headed females
25% Black-headed females

15. *Black-headed × Yellow-headed*
50% Red-headed/Black-headed and Yellow-headed males
50% Black-headed/Yellow-headed females

16. *Black-headed × Black-headed/Yellow-headed*
25% Black-headed/Yellow-headed males
25% Black-headed males
25% Black-headed/Yellow-headed females
25% Black-headed females

17. *Black-headed × Black-headed with yellow bill*
50% Black-headed/Yellow-headed males
50% Black-headed/Yellow-headed females

18. *Black-headed × Black-headed*
50% Black-headed males
50% Black-headed females

19. *Black-headed/Yellow-headed × Red-headed*
25% Red-headed/Black-headed males
25% Black-headed/Yellow-headed females
25%Red-headed/Black-headed and Yellow-headed males
25% Black-headed females

20. *Black-headed/Yellow-headed × Red-headed/Yellow-headed*
16⁶⁄₇% Red-headed/Black-headed males
16⁶⁄₇% Black-headed/Yellow-headed females
16⁶⁄₇% Red-headed/Black-headed and Yellow-headed females
16⁶⁄₇% Black-headed females
16⁶⁄₇% Yellow-headed/Black-headed males
16⁶⁄₇% Black-headed/Black-headed with yellow bill females

21. *Black-headed/Yellow-headed × Yellow-headed*
25% Red-headed/Black-headed and Yellow-headed males
25% Black-headed/Yellow-headed females
25% Yellow-headed/Black-headed males
25% Black-headed/Black-headed with yellow bill females

22. *Black-headed/Yellow-headed × Black-headed*
25% Black-headed/Yellow-headed males
25% Black-headed/Yellow-headed females
25% Black-headed males
25% Black-headed females

23. *Black-headed/Yellow-headed × Black-headed/Yellow- headed*

16⅔% Black-headed/Yellow-headed males
16⅔% Black-headed/Yellow-headed females
16⅔% Black-headed males
16⅔% Black-headed females
16⅔% Black-headed/Black-headed with yellow bill males
16⅔% Black-headed/Black-headed with yellow bill females
24. *Black-headed/Yellow-headed × Black-headed/Black-headed with yellow bill*
25% Black-headed/Yellow-headed males
25% Black-headed/Yellow-headed females
25% Black-headed/Black-headed with yellow bill males
25% Black-headed/Black-headed with yellow bill females
25. *Black-headed/Black-headed with yellow bill × Red-headed*
50% Red-headed/Black-headed and Yellow-headed males
Black-headed/Yellow-headed females
26. *Black-headed/Black-headed with yellow bill × Red-headed/Yellow-headed*
25% Black-headed/Black-headed and Yellow-headed males
25% Black-headed/Yellow-headed females
25% Yellow-headed/Black-headed males
25% Red-headed/Black-headed with yellow bill females
27. *Black-headed/Black-headed with yellow bill × Yellow-headed*
50% Yellow-headed/Black-headed males
50% Black-headed/Black-headed with yellow bill females
28. *Black-headed/Black-headed with yellow bill × Black-headed*
50% Black-headed/Yellow-headed males
50% Black-headed/Yellow-headed females
29. *Black-headed/Black-headed with yellow bill × Black-headed/Yellow-headed*
25% Black-headed/Yellow-headed males
25% Black-headed/Yellow-headed females
25% Black-headed/Black-headed with yellow bill males
25% Black-headed/Black-headed with yellow bill females
30. *Black-headed/Black-headed with yellow bill × Black-headed/Black-headed with yellow bill*
50% Black-headed/Black-headed with yellow bill males
50% Black-headed/Black-headed with yellow bill females
31. *Red-headed × Red-headed*
50% Red-headed males
50% Red-headed females
32. *Red-headed × Red-headed/Yellow-headed*
25% Red-headed males
25% Red-headed females
25% Red-headed/Yellow-headed males
25% Red-headed/Yellow-headed females
33. *Red-headed × Yellow-headed*
50% Red-headed/Yellow-headed males
50% Red-headed/Yellow-headed females
34. *Red-headed × Black-headed*
50% Red-headed/Black-headed males
50% Red-headed females
35. *Red-headed × Black-headed/Yellow-headed*

25% Red-headed/Black-headed males
25% Red-headed females
25% Red-headed/Black-headed and Yellow-headed males
25% Red-headed/Yellow-headed females
36. *Red-headed × Black-headed/Black-headed with yellow bill*
50% Red-headed/Black-headed and Yellow-headed males
50% Red-headed/Yellow-headed females
37. *Red-headed/Yellow-headed × Red-headed*
25% Red-headed males
25% Red-headed females
25% Red-headed/Yellow-headed males
25% Red-headed/Yellow-headed females
38. *Red-headed/Yellow-headed × Red-headed/Yellow-headed*
16⅔% Red-headed males
16⅔% Red-headed females
16⅔% Red-headed/Yellow-headed males
16⅔% Red-headed/Yellow-headed females
16⅔% Yellow-headed males
16⅔% Yellow-headed females
39. *Red-headed/Yellow-headed × Yellow-headed*
25% Red-headed/Yellow-headed males
25% Red-headed/Yellow-headed females
25% Yellow-headed males
25% Yellow-headed females
40. *Red-headed/Yellow-headed × Black-headed*
25% Red-headed/Black-headed males
25% Red-headed females
25% Red-headed/Black-headed and Yellow-headed males
25% Red-headed/Yellow-headed females
41. *Red-headed/Yellow-headed × Black-headed/Yellow-headed*
16⅔% Red-headed/Black-headed males
16⅔% Red-headed females
16⅔% Yellow-headed/Black-headed males
16⅔% Yellow-headed females
16⅔% Red-headed/Black-headed and Yellow-headed males
16⅔% Red-headed/Yellow-headed females
42. *Red-headed/Yellow-headed × Black-headed with yellow bill*
25% Red-headed/Black-headed and Yellow-headed males
25% Red-headed/Yellow-headed females
25% Yellow-headed/Black-headed males
25% Yellow-headed females
43. *Red-headed/Black-headed × Red-headed*
25% Red-headed males
25% Red-headed females
25% Red-headed/Black-headed males
25% Black-headed females
44. *Red-headed/Black-headed × Red-headed/Yellow-headed*
12½% Red-headed males
12½% Red-headed females
12½% Red-headed/Yellow-headed males
12½% Red-headed/Yellow-headed females
12½% Red-headed/Black-headed males
12½% Black-headed females

Matings List

12½% Red-headed/Black-headed and Yellow-headed males
12½% Black-headed/Yellow-headed females
45. Red-headed/Black-headed × Yellow-headed
25% Red-headed/Yellow-headed males
25% Red-headed/Yellow-headed females
25% Red-headed/Black-headed and Yellow-headed males
25% Black-headed/Yellow-headed females
46. Red-headed/Black-headed × Black-headed
25% Red-headed/Black-headed males
25% Red-headed females
25% Black-headed males
25% Black-headed females
47. Red-headed/Black-headed × Black-headed/Yellow-headed
12½% Red-headed/Black-headed males
12½% Red-headed females
12½% Red-headed/Black-headed and Yellow-headed males
12½% Red-headed/Yellow-headed females
12½% Black-headed/Yellow-headed males
12½% Black-headed/Yellow-headed females
12½% Black-headed males
12½% Black-headed females
48. Red-headed/Black-headed × Black-headed/Black-headed with yellow bill
25% Red-headed/Black-headed and Yellow-headed males
25% Red-headed/Yellow-headed females
25% Black-headed/Yellow-headed males
25% Black-headed/Yellow-headed females
49. Red-headed/Black-headed and Yellow-headed × Red-headed
12½% Red-headed males
12½% Red-headed females
12½% Red-headed/Yellow-headed males
12½% Red-headed/Yellow-headed females
12½% Red-headed/Black-headed males
12½% Black-headed/Yellow-headed females
12½% Red-headed/Black-headed and Yellow-headed males
12½% Black-headed females
50. Red-headed/Black-headed and Yellow-headed × Red-headed/Yellow-headed
8⅓% Red-headed males
8⅓% Red-headed females
8⅓% Red-headed/Yellow-headed males
8⅓% Red-headed/Yellow-headed females
8⅓% Yellow-headed males
8⅓% Yellow-headed females
8⅓% Yellow-headed/Black-headed males
8⅓% Black-headed/Yellow-headed females
8⅓% Red-headed/Black-headed males

8⅓% Black-headed females
8⅓% Red-headed/Black-headed and Yellow-headed males
8⅓% Black-headed/Black-headed with yellow bill females
51. Red-headed/Black-headed and Yellow-headed × Yellow-headed
12½% Red-headed/Yellow-headed males
12½% Red-headed/Yellow-headed females
12½% Yellow-headed males
12½% Yellow-headed females
12½% Yellow-headed/Black-headed males
12½% Black-headed/Yellow-headed females
12½% Red-headed/Black-headed and Yellow-headed males
12½% Black-headed/Black-headed with yellow bill females
52. Red-headed/Black-headed and Yellow-headed × Black-headed
12½% Red-headed/Black-headed males
12½% Red-headed females
12½% Red-headed/Black-headed and Yellow-headed males
12½% Red-headed/Yellow-headed females
12½% Black-headed/Yellow-headed males
12½% Black-headed/Yellow-headed females
12½% Black-headed males
12½% Black-headed females
53. Black-headed/Black-headed and Yellow-headed × Black-headed/Yellow-headed
8⅓% Red-headed/Black-headed males
8⅓% Red-headed females
8⅓% Red-headed/Black-headed and Yellow-headed males
8⅓% Red-headed/Yellow-headed females
8⅓% Yellow-headed/Black-headed males
8⅓% Yellow-headed females
8⅓% Black-headed/Yellow-headed males
8⅓% Black-headed/Yellow-headed females
8⅓% Black-headed males
8⅓% Black-headed females
8⅓% Black-headed/Black-headed with yellow bill males
8⅓% Black-headed/Black-headed with yellow bill females
54. Black-headed/Black-headed and Yellow-headed × Black-headed/Black-headed with yellow bill
12½% Red-headed/Black-headed and Yellow-headed males
12½% Red-headed/Yellow-headed females
12½% Yellow-headed/Black-headed males
12½% Yellow-headed females
12½% Black-headed/Yellow-headed males
12½% Black-headed/Yellow-headed females
12½% Black-headed/Black-headed with yellow bill males
12½% Black-headed/Black-headed with yellow bill females

Literature and Addresses

Magazines

American Cage Bird Magazine
One Glamore Court
Smithtown, New York 11787

Avicultural Magazine
Journal of the Avicultural Society
c/o Windsor Forest Stud
Mill Ride
Berkshire, SL5 8LT
England

Bird Talk
P.O. Box 6050
Mission Viejo, California 92690

Bird World
P.O. Box 70
N. Hollywood, California 91603

The A.F.A. Watchbird
Journal of the American Federation of
Aviculture
2208 "A" Artesia Boulevard
Redondo Beach, California 90278

The Canary & Finch Journal
P.O. Box 1583
Lake Oswego, Oregon 97035

*Journal of the Association of Avian
Veterinarians*
5770 Lake Worth Road
Lake Worth, Florida 33463-3299

Organizations

Association of Avian Veterinarians
P.O. Box 299
East Northport, New York 11731

National Finch & Softbill Society
125 W. Jackson St.
York, Pennsylvania 17403

Books

Evans, S. and M. Fidler. *The Gouldian Finch.* Blandford Press, London, New York, Sydney, 1986.

Goodwin, Derek. *Estrildid Finches of the World.* British Museum (Natural History)/Oxford University Press, London and Oxford, 1982.

Immelmann, K. *Australian Finches in Bush and Aviary.* Angus and Robertson, Sydney; revised edition, 1982.

Koepff, C. *The New Finch Handbook.* Barron's Educational Series, Inc., Hauppauge, New York, 1984.

Mobbs, A. J. "A New Mutation of the Gouldian Finch." *Avicultural Magazine.* London, Vol. 83/1983.

— —. *Gouldian Finches.* Nimrod Book Service, Liss, Hants, England, 1985.

Pomarede, M. "Diamant de Gould à poitrine rose." *Le Journal des Oiseaux,* 4/1983.

— —. "Diamant de Gould bleu ." *Le Journal des Oiseaux,* 11/1983.

— —. "Mutations gould." *Le Journal des Oiseaux,* 11/1982.

Reader's Digest Complete Book of Australian Birds. Reader's Digest Services PTY Ltd. Sydney, 1976.

Teague, P. W. "Experiences in removal and feeding methods." *Avicultural Magazine,* London, 1936.

— —. "Gouldians." *Avicultural Magazine,* London, 1933.

— —. "Gouldian Finches." *Avicultural Magazine,* London, 1932.

— —. "Some Experiences with Gouldian Finches." *Avicultural Magazine,* London, 1931.

Index

Index

"A solid bet for first-time pet owners"
—*Booklist*

We've taken all the best features of our popular Pet Owner's Manuals and added *more* expert advice, *more* sparkling color photographs, *more* fascinating behavioral insights, and fact-filled profiles on the leading breeds. Indispensable references for pet owners, ideal for people who want to compare breeds before choosing a pet. Over 120 illustrations per book – 55 to 60 in full color!

"*Stunning*"
– Roger Caras
Pets & Wildlife

THE NEW AQUARIUM HANDBOOK, Scheurmann (3682-4)
THE NEW AUSTRALIAN PARAKEET HANDBOOK, Vriends (4739-7)
THE NEW BIRD HANDBOOK, Vriends (4157-7)
THE NEW CANARY HANDBOOK, Vriends (4879-2)
THE NEW CAT HANDBOOK, Müller (2922-4)
THE NEW CHAMELEONS HANDBOOK, Le Berre (1805-2)
THE NEW COCKATIEL HANDBOOK, Vriends (4201-8)
THE NEW DOG HANDBOOK, H.J. Ullmann (2857-0)
THE NEW DUCK HANDBOOK, Raethel (4088-0)
THE NEW FINCH HANDBOOK, Koepff (2859-7)
THE NEW GOAT HANDBOOK, Jaudas (4090-2)
THE NEW PARAKEET HANDBOOK, Birmelin / Wolter (2985-2)
THE NEW PARROT HANDBOOK, Lantermann (3729-4)
THE NEW RABBIT HANDBOOK, Vriends-Parent (4202-6)
THE NEW SALTWATER AQUARIUM HANDBOOK, Blasiola (4482-7)
THE NEW SOFTBILL HANDBOOK, W. Steinigeweg (4075-9)
THE NEW TERRIER HANDBOOK, Kern (3951-3)

Barron's Educational Series, Inc.
250 Wireless Blvd., Hauppauge, NY 11788
In Canada: Georgetown Book Warehouse
34 Armstrong Ave., Georgetown, Ont. L7G 4R9
Barron's ISBN prefix: 0-8120   (#63) R3/96
Order from your favorite bookstore or pet shop.